ncfe handbook to

Understanding, Preparing for, and Responding to Challenges to Your Freedom of Artistic Expression

NATIONAL CAMPAIGN FOR FREEDOM OF EXPRESSION

Printed in the United States.

Library of Congress 98-067316

Cover and interior design by Cutting Edge Graphics

ISBN 0-9666029-0-0

Table of Contents

NCFE

THE NATIONAL CAMPAIGN FOR FREEDOM OF EXPRESSION

Assisting artists and organizations facing challenges to their freedom of artistic expression is at the core of NCFE's mission. NCFE was founded in 1990 in response to attacks on the National Endowment for the Arts and the National Endowment for the Humanities. The organization originated as a weekly conference call among arts activists who were concerned that arts organizations were trading basic principles of artistic freedom for their own financial survival. In these calls, founding members of NCFE discovered that challenges to artistic freedom were occurring at local, as well as national, levels.

Inspired by the politically charged frenzy around the public funding of institutions that presented works by visual artists Robert Mapplethorpe and Andres Serrano, self-appointed guardians of the public morals in cities and towns across America organized to defund and shut down exhibitions and performances they considered—for whatever reason—obscene, seditious, immoral, or offensive. Few of these attacks received national press coverage, and artists were often left to fend for themselves, their rights largely ignored.

NCFE established a hotline for artists and organizations under attack and began publishing the *National Campaign for Freedom of Expression Quarterly*, a compilation of censorship incidents and ongoing discussions of freedom of expression issues. By providing resources, information, and technical assistance, NCFE has empowered artists and arts organizations to help themselves, enabling them to mobilize their own communities in defense of artistic freedom. Since 1990, NCFE has helped over 200 artists and organizations fight back against challenges to artistic freedom.

Foreword

Understanding, Preparing for, and Responding to Challenges to Your Freedom of Artistic Expression

by David C. Mendoza
Executive Director, NCFE, 1991–1997

This handbook is the result of seven years of NCFE's front-line experience helping artists and organizations that have faced threats to their freedom of artistic expression. The urge to censor is hardly new, and the means of censorship are varied. NCFE has worked to redress many cases of overt censorship—canceled performances, withdrawal of public funding, removal of books from library shelves—but censorship also occurs more covertly.

Institutional censorship has had an impact on artists and cultural groups producing work considered at or outside the margins of "mainstream" society. Publishing houses, foundations, record companies, art galleries, movie studios, and museums, have historically been controlled by Caucasian men who haven't always been welcoming to artists of color, women, or out gays and lesbians. NCFE has been an active participant in public policy discussions, educational forums, and the media, educating the public about and advocating for continued progress toward eliminating institutional censorship.

At the end of the twentieth century, support for artists and cultures outside the mainstream has vastly improved. One precipitating factor of this change is also at the root of the threats to freedom of artistic expression today: public funding for culture.

In 1965, President Lyndon Johnson signed legislation authorizing the National Endowments for the Arts and Humanities. Since then public funding for the arts and humanities has expanded, and today there are arts agencies in every state and territory, and in hundreds of county and municipal governments. There are also humanities commissions or councils in every state. Taxpayers have been serving as patrons of the arts and humanities for over thirty years.

With this public support came the imperative to recognize the rich artistic diversity of the people, cultures, and communities that make up America. Nonprofit organizations and artists that had never been the beneficiaries of philanthropy received not only financial support but also the imprimatur of respected public agencies such as the National Endowment for the Arts. This respect was conferred by the peer panel process through which arts professionals adjudicate and award grants of public dollars to their peers. This process is a singular and powerful contribution to cultural democracy in America. There has been far more diversity in the NEA peer panels than in the Congress that has recently derided them. Peer panels—which change with each round of grant requests—have served to insulate the grantmaking process from political pressure by elected officials and even, to large extent, by the members of the granting commissions appointed by the president, governors, and mayors.

Public funding of the arts and humanities has been a key factor in the diversification of American cultural life. This move to diversify support for arts programs was a political imperative for public agencies because the money is contributed by all taxpayers, who could expect (unlike in corporate or private philanthropy at the time) to be represented on the staffs, panels, and appointed commissions, as well as in the organizations that received public funding. Slowly but steadily, these agencies have nurtured cultural expression reflecting a far broader range of national experience than was generally portrayed before 1960. The rise of public arts funding took place concurrently with the rise of the civil rights, women's, and gay and lesbian rights movements. As a result, we now can enjoy a rich gumbo of cultural and personal artistic expressions that did not exist before 1960. Ballet Hispanico (New York City), Northwest Asian American Theatre (Seattle), San Francisco Gay and Lesbian Film Festival, National Black Arts Festival (Atlanta), California Indian Basketweavers Association, and Women Make Art (Austin) are a tiny sampling of the organizations that have received public funding from the NEA and local arts agencies. A list of individual artists who have received public support would yield a similar diversity. The culture of America has finally begun to "look like America." Multiculturalism is neither rhetoric nor a political position; it is a reality as we move into the next millennium.

Perhaps inevitably, there was a backlash from those who felt threatened by a multicultural America. Since 1989 the arts community has faced an escalating attack on freedom of artistic expression. In the spring of that year Robert Mapplethorpe (a gay photographer whose work included images of sadomasochism) and Andres Serrano (a photographer of Afro-Caribbean descent whose *Piss Christ* featured a plastic crucifix in a jar of urine) became the first targets in what has become known as the culture war. First denounced by the then little-known "religious right," these "blasphemous" and transgressive images—some presentations of which were funded in small part by public tax dollars—presented a significant political opportunity for Senator Jesse Helms (R-NC) and his conservative cohorts.

The established arts community did not exactly leap to the front lines to defend against these broadsides from the right. Some thought the controversy would "blow over" quickly, others felt that the Mapplethorpe and Serrano works were too difficult to defend, and still others did not wish to risk their own funding to champion art at the margins. The silence of mainstream cultural organizations was, in fact, as deafening as the cries of outrage from the other side. In the face of the controversy, the Corcoran Gallery in Washington, D.C., canceled the Mapplethorpe exhibit because the gallery feared funding reprisal from Congress. That decision revealed an arts establishment vulnerable to attack. The fault lines were clear.

In response to this leadership vacuum, the National Campaign for Freedom of Expression was created in 1990 by artists, arts activists, and administrators of the organizations who had supported, produced, and presented the works of artists under attack. Support also came from funders and colleagues in the civil liberties community who had a history of supporting cultural diversity and fighting censorship. One of the first actions of NCFE was to initiate a lawsuit against the NEA in 1990 on behalf of four artists (John Fleck, Karen Finley, Holly Hughes, and Tim Miller) whose grants had been denied by then–NEA chair John Frohnmayer from fear of a Congressional funding reprisal. Several months later the suit was amended to include a constitutional challenge to the "standards of decency" clause which Congress included in the reauthorization language of the NEA. Part of the suit was settled out of court in 1993 in favor of the four artists whose grants were reinstated. A federal district court ruled the "decency" language unconstitutional in 1992, and the Clinton administration appealed that decision. An appeals court upheld the district court ruling in November 1997. The administration appealed to the Supreme Court which heard the case in March 1998. In June 1998, the Supreme Court held that the language was constitutional as a factor in determining artistic merit but not as a standard for a categorical prohibition against funding "indecent" or "disrespectful" art.

One unfortunate result of the lower courts' rulings against the "standards of decency," was that the chair and members of the NEA's National Council on the Arts learned to *publicly* talk about "artistic merit" when, in fact, their real concern was still the content. Although NEA spokespersons claimed otherwise, recorded transcripts of an August 1994 meeting of the council revealed that a decision to reject fellowships in photography for Andres Serrano, Barbara DeGenevieve, and Merry Alpern (fellowships that had been recommended by the peer panel) was motivated by concerns that there might be further political problems because of the content of the work. Council members also wanted to signal irate members of Congress that the NEA was paying attention to their outrage.

A rise of less well publicized challenges to artistic freedom has occurred throughout the nation, many examples of which are included in this handbook. Artistic freedom is threatened by well-intentioned arts officials who have grown nervous about potential controversy. It is not uncommon for an exhibit director to ponder the selection of a particular work of art based on its potential for generating controversy rather than on its artistic merit. Arts organizations valiantly defend freedom of expression in the face of a controversial program, and afterwards artistic directors or curators are warned by board members or funders "to be careful" in the future. And many artists, fearing they will not get a grant or commission or will be excluded from a exhibition, submit work they think conforms to some vague notion of decency standards. The true chilling effect of censorship is self-censorship. Danilo Kis, the late Czech writer, wrote in *HomoPoeticus* (1985):

> *Invisible but here, far from the public eye and buried deep in the most secret parts of the spirit, [self-censorship] is far more efficient than censorship. While both depend on the same means — threats, fear, blackmail — self-censorship masks, or at any rate does not reveal the exercise of, constraint. The fight against censorship is open and dangerous and thus heroic, while the battle against self-*

censorship is anonymous, lonely, and unwitnessed — a source of humiliation and shame for the collaborator. Self-censorship means reading your own text through someone else's eyes, a situation that makes you your own judge. You become stricter and more suspicious than anyone else could, because you know what no censor could ever discover — your most secret, unspoken thoughts...

The war on the arts and culture is really a war on critical thinking, dissent, risk-taking, creativity, and democracy. With disinformation, sound bites, and defamation of character, conservatives have demonized artists, transforming them in the public mind into blasphemers and pornographers. Ironically, many of the artists who have been defunded and defamed for being immoral are in fact communicating a moral vision. It is just that their art, appropriately—though disparagingly—labeled "political," is critical, unflinching, and often dissenting against the majority.

Often all it takes for a piece of art to be censored is for one person to complain that he or she finds it offensive. It has become almost a criminal act to offend someone. Expressing criticism of a controversial work — often without even seeing it — is not enough for some people; because they are offended they don't want anyone else to have access to the art. Perhaps they fear others will be offended. Perhaps they think others should be offended. But offending and dissenting are not only permissible but should be celebrated in a democratic society.

The great Japanese filmmaker Akira Kurosawa said, "Being an artist means never to avert one's eyes." I believe our challenge is not to avert our eyes from what artists see. And even if our religious or political beliefs compel us to avert our eyes we must, in a democracy, resist the urge to enforce our choice on others.

As you review the material in this handbook, either as preparation for the possibility of facing a censorship challenge or because you are now in the midst of one, be clear about what you are risking and what you are fighting for. Speaking out or taking action against censorship can mean going against a prevailing or majority opinion; it can make an artist a pariah in his or her own community, even among other artists. If you are a bystander, this handbook will help you support the artist or organization in your community that stands up to threats of censorship. These battles are about the promise of liberty, equality, and democracy guaranteed by the Constitution and the Bill of Rights for all Americans. These battles are about values: the value of respect for individual and cultural diversity in a nation of native peoples, immigrants, and descendants of immigrants. The value of intellectual freedom, critical thinking, and dissent in a world where fundamentalist militants and totalitarian regimes imprison and/or issue death threats against artists and journalists; and the value of artists and intellectuals in a free society.

At the close of 1997, I end my tenure at NCFE with enormous respect for those individuals who have had the courage to stand up for freedom of expression, sometimes with little support, and even in the face of hostility in their own communities. We are all indebted to you.

Comment

This document represents the work of many individuals who have been involved with the Freedom of Expression struggle much longer than NCFE's humble beginnings in 1990. We realize in releasing this manual we are carrying forward the work that others have done before us. It is our hope that the value to be found in the practical use of this manual will be shared by artists, arts organizations, gallery owners, museum curators, free expression organizations, and the general public.

We dedicate this publication to those who continue the struggle in artistic free expression circles, to those whose hearts remain in the free expression struggle and finally, to those who struggle quietly and courageously in their own communities. The visual artist at work in his or her studio or living room carries forth a vision. The dancer who choreographs a dance piece that challenges and moves the audience and the performance artist who looks into his or her own experience and finds a channel for that experience on a stage or in a private space do as well. These artists will often walk down a lonely or muddled path.

We want this manual to remind those individuals or organizations who continue to impose their divisive morality on the individual artist, the dance troupe, or the theater group as a challenge to our democratic ideals of free expression that our visions will carry forth regardless of the barriers placed in our paths. Artists have been targeted as the first to face censorship or eradication in revolutions throughout world history. The artist survives because the vision survives.

Gary D. Schwartz
Executive Director

Introduction

Freedom of artistic expression is the principle that an artist should be unrestrained by law or convention in the making of his or her art. Artistic freedom is vital to both the cultural and political health of our society. It is essential in a democracy that values and protects the rights of the individual to espouse his or her beliefs.

Just as our nation's free speech heritage protects the rights of artists to create, display, perform, and sell their artwork, so too does it protect the rights of the general public to dislike, criticize, and be offended by artwork. What we will call a "challenge" to the freedom of artistic expression is more than mere criticism or commentary. A "challenge" arises when the critic takes the significant leap from merely voicing distaste of the art to questioning its right to exist or be seen, and seeking to stop its exhibition or performance.

Artistic freedom is threatened when art is challenged because of its content, message or viewpoint, rather than because of its aesthetic qualities or artistic merit. A challenge may be motivated by disagreement with the perceived message or the fear of negative public reaction. A challenge may be part of an organized effort to protest specific social issues. Challenges may come from members of the general public, representatives of organizations, or governmental officials. Challenges may also originate from within the arts community—for example, from curators, artistic directors, or funders.

Although most challenges to artistic freedom share common themes, each circumstance is shaped by unique facts and nuances. This handbook provides artists, arts presenters, and audience members with an historical and legal context for understanding, preparing for, and responding to challenges to artistic freedom, and suggests preparation, coping, and response strategies for the typical incident. This handbook is but a beginning. In the event you are faced with a challenge to your freedom of artistic expression, seek out additional advice and assistance.

The Problematic Rhetoric of "Censorship"

It is easy to get caught in the trap of debating whether a challenge to your freedom of artistic expression is or is not "censorship." Some argue that "censorship" refers only to governmental, as opposed to private, action. And the implication is often that if it is not "censorship," the artist has no real grounds for recourse or complaint. Rather than becoming entangled in these unhelpful semantic tussles, this handbook uses the term "challenges" to refer to all assaults on freedom of artistic expression, whether by government or by private organizations and individuals. The term "censorship" is reserved for actions by governmental employees acting in their official capacities.

CHAPTER 1

Understanding, Preparing for, and Responding to Challenges to Your Freedom of Artistic Expression

This handbook focuses on the three most common types of challenges to freedom of artistic expression: protests and boycotts, breaches of exhibition contracts, and censorship by governmental officials. A single incident may involve any one or combination of these challenges.

Protests & Boycotts

Protests by private organizations or individuals, offended either by the presentation of art or the mere fact of its existence, often prove to be the most disruptive challenge. Even when the artist has the support of the presenter, local government officials, and the majority of the community, offended and organized individuals can effectively disrupt an exhibition or performance. Tactics range from staged demonstrations to extensive media campaigns and organized boycotts of the presentation and its financial backers.

Challenges to artistic freedom often come from organized segments of what has become known as the "religious right." Most of the well-known national organizations, such as the Christian Coalition, the American Family Association, and Focus on the Family, have local chapters that may actively monitor art in your community. Some conservative church and parents organizations may also devote energy and financial resources to challenging artistic freedom.

But such challenges do not originate exclusively from the right side of the political spectrum. Some organizations and individuals identifying with the left

Distinguish Between "Challenges" & Artistic Decisions

It is important to distinguish between censorial and curatorial decisions. Decisions made by arts professionals, based on considerations of merit, to exclude a work of art from a particular presentation are not challenges to artistic freedom. Of course, the distinction between a censorial and curatorial decision is not always clear, and artistic quality is often cited by challengers when they are actually reacting to the content, message, or viewpoint of the art.

are also active proponents of restraints on artistic freedom. For example, certain artwork dealing with race or ethnicity has been characterized as hate speech by some civil rights organizations, and some women's rights activists have spoken out against art that depicts women in sexual situations.

Protesters Destroy Jock Sturges's Books

In the fall of 1997, protesters in several cities across the country entered Barnes & Noble and Borders bookstores and destroyed copies of books by acclaimed photographer Jock Sturges. The books contained photographs of nude children and young adults. These local protests were part of a national effort to encourage local prosecutors to press charges against the bookstores for distributing child pornography. Spearheading the national effort were James Dobson of Focus on the Family and Randall Terry, former head of the anti–reproductive rights organization Operation Rescue, who used their nationally broadcast radio programs to encourage the protesters. Books were destroyed in approximately ten locations and large, disruptive protests took place in numerous others. The protests prompted prosecutors in at least two states to file criminal charges against the booksellers.

FIGURE 1
The Dream Deferred
Barbara Bullock & Lee Ann Mitchell

Complaints from Passersby Prompt Removal of "Racially Insensitive" Display

In October 1993, *The Dream Deferred* (Fig. 1), by Lee Ann Mitchell and the late Barbara Bullock, was removed from display by the owner of a downtown Memphis office building following complaints from passersby that the piece was "racist" and "offensive." The work was part of a public art series placed in storefronts along the route of the 1968 Memphis sanitation workers strike to commemorate the strike and the assassination of Dr. Martin Luther King, Jr. It included two doll-like caricatures—one black, the other white—lynched from a tree set against a backdrop of garbage. Bullock, who was African-American, created the black figure, and Mitchell, who is white, created the white figure.

Breach of Exhibition Contract

Artistic freedom is also challenged when a presenter or site manager backs out of an agreement to present art because of the content or viewpoint of the work. The atmosphere of controversy surrounding the arts in recent years has created a cautionary urge to avoid conflict or loss of funding on the part of some presenters.

The presenter may be a private organization or a governmental body such as a city hall or public university art gallery.

Governmental Action

Federal, state, and local government has vast capacity to protect, enhance, or restrict freedom of artistic expression. The government controls the use of public performance and exhibition spaces and regulates broadcast and telecommunications media. The government funds the arts directly and indirectly. And the government may enact laws that directly or indirectly restrict the creation or exhibition of art, even if the art is produced for private purposes and exhibited privately.

It is important to note that what the government is legally entitled to do, what it will do, and what it should do as a matter of public policy are very often not the same. If you believe the government has acted unlawfully, you may be able to get relief through litigation. However, even lawful government actions need not go uncontested.

Art is Constitutionally Protected Speech

Art Is "Speech"

Art and artistic expression are considered "speech" and are thus constitutionally protected by the First Amendment to the United States Constitution. Although the First Amendment very strongly limits the government's ability to restrict artistic expression, the limitations are not absolute. In many circumstances the government is permitted some control over artistic expression.

Sifting Through the Legal Mumbo Jumbo

The discussion of legal concepts included in this handbook is a very basic framing of some of the issues that commonly arise with challenges to artistic freedom. This handbook is not intended to provide definitive guidance on legal questions; this area of the law is actively evolving and may vary significantly from state to state. Whether or not an artist or arts organization has a legal claim against a challenger depends upon the specific context and facts of the situation. Consult a lawyer if you suspect that the government may have violated your First Amendment rights to freedom of artistic expression. See Appendix II for a list of organizations that can refer you to legal support.

The First Amendment

Congress shall make no law respecting an establishment of religion, or prohibiting the free exercise thereof; or abridging the freedom of speech, or of the press, or the right of the people peaceably to assemble, and to petition the Government for a redress of grievances.

Vagueness

When government acts to regulate expression, it must do so in a way that is not vague or unclear to either those who must administer the regulation or those who are bound by it. Regulations with uncertain reach may be deemed unconstitutional if they have the strong potential to chill constitutionally protected artistic expression. For example, an ordinance prohibiting "controversial" performance at a park amphitheater would likely be unconstitutionally vague because the category of expression barred was not defined precisely enough and performers would curtail their expression more than necessary in order to ensure they did not present something "controversial." As a result of this vagueness, enforcement of the ordinance would be left up to the personal preferences and predilections of those enforcing it.

"If you can control representation of the body, you can control the body politic. That's why we fight censorship."

Marilyn Zimmerman, *photographer*

Some Types of Speech Are Entitled to More Protection Than Others

All speech is not treated with equal respect under the First Amendment. Generally, political speech is entitled to the greatest constitutional protection, and advertising—commonly identified as "commercial speech"—is entitled to the least. Most other forms of speech fall somewhere in between. In some situations, courts deciding the legality of a restriction on free speech balance the value of the speech against the importance of the governmental interest the restriction on expression is intended to serve. Expression that is considered by courts to be on the "margins of constitutional protection," such as go-go dancing, may have little weight in these balancing tests.

Unprotected Forms of Expression

Some forms of speech are not entitled to any constitutional protection at all. The government's ability to prohibit and regulate these categories of expression is not limited by the First Amendment.

OBSCENITY

Obscenity is defined as speech that, when considered as a whole, appeals to a prurient or morbid interest in sex (based on "community standards"), depicts or describes in a patently offensive manner (again, according to local community standards) sexual conduct or organs specifically defined by the applicable law, and, considered in its whole form, is devoid of serious literary, artistic, political, or scientific value. If art with acknowledged artistic value violates community standards, it may be considered "indecent," but it is not "obscene." "Indecent" material is protected by the First Amendment (although it may be considered to be "on the margins" of protected speech). "Pornography," which has no precise definition but is commonly used to describe material with explicit sexual content, is not a legal term and should not be used interchangeably with "obscenity."

CHILD PORNOGRAPHY

Child pornography is the lewd visual depiction of the genitalia of minors or any visual depiction of minors engaged in sexual activity. This determination is made without reference to community standards of decency. The Supreme Court has not decided whether it is relevant that the work as a whole have any literary, artistic, political, or scientific value. A 1996 federal law bans images simulating minors in graphic sexual activity (using computer-generated images or young-looking adults). The law is currently being challenged in the courts. Child pornography laws vary significantly from state to state. Federal law defines a "minor" as any person under 18.

Fine Art Photographers Charged with Child Pornography

It is not uncommon for challengers to tag depictions of nude children in nonsexual situations as "child pornography." Both fine art and amateur family photographers and filmmakers have been subject to child pornography investigations and prosecutions. In November 1994, Tucson police seized a photograph by acclaimed photographer Robyn McDaniels and charged her with violating Arizona's sexual exploitation of a minor law. The photograph depicted McDaniels's nude four-year-old son holding a decapitated chicken so that it partially obscured his genitals. The charges were dropped after McDaniels allowed the deputy county attorney to keep the photograph. McDaniels retained the negative, several prints, and all rights to the image.

FIGURE 2
Details from Marilyn Zimmerman's Proof Sheets

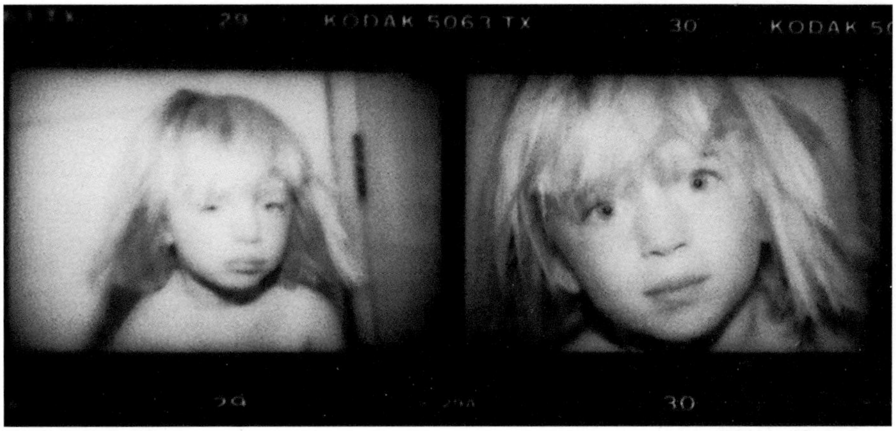

In December 1994, Marilyn Zimmerman, a noted photographer and professor of art at Wayne State University in Detroit, was the subject of a child pornography investigation after police came across a proof sheet that Zimmerman had discarded. The proof sheet included five black and white images of Zimmerman's three-year-old daughter as she emerged from a bathtub (Fig. 2). In some of the images, Zimmerman's daughter was touching her genitals. The police interrogated Zimmerman, searched her office and home, and confiscated approximately 250 photographs. Prosecutors decided not to press charges after they received numerous letters of support for Zimmerman from artists, art schools, and arts organizations around the country attesting to the artistic merit of her work. Six weeks after the charges were dropped, the Michigan legislature voted 95-5 to remove the clause from the Michigan child pornography law that set out an exception for works created with artistic intent.

A New Jersey businessman was jailed on child endangerment charges after a photography lab turned over to police pictures he had taken of his nude six-year-old daughter for a photography class. Ejlat Feuer was handcuffed, jailed, and barred from his home and all contact with his daughter for two months. Processing labs in New Jersey, and several other states, are required to report to police any suspicious photographs of minors. The charges were eventually dropped.

Oklahoma Judge Finds *Tin Drum* Obscene

In 1997, police in Oklahoma City seized copies of Volker Schlondorff's Academy Award–winning film *The Tin Drum* from video stores, libraries, and one private home after a judge informally ruled that a scene from the film was illegal under an Oklahoma obscenity law that includes child pornography. The scene implied that a child briefly performed oral sex on a 17-year-old woman.

"HARMFUL TO MINORS"

Art not considered legally obscene for adults may nevertheless be defined as "obscene to minors" or "harmful to minors." Lawmakers may prevent youth under 17 from receiving material—except from their parents—that predominantly appeals to unwholesome sexual interests of minors, is patently offensive to the prevailing standards of the adult community as to what is suitable for minors, and is devoid of any serious value for minors. Generally, not every depiction of nudity can be deemed "harmful to minors," but sexually graphic language alone may qualify. States commonly restrict the placement and display of these materials to ensure that only adults can access them. For example, a law may prevent art books featuring adult material from being sold to minors or displayed in such a way that minors can easily peruse them.

Display on Private Property Leads to Harmful to Minors Charge

In October 1995, a neighbor and a local minister filed a citizen's criminal complaint against New Mexico sculptor Candyce Garrett, claiming that the artist had displayed sexually explicit material to minors. Garrett had worked on

Rapture (Fig. 3) on the patio outside her studio. The sculpture was visible from the sidewalk. The district attorney dismissed the complaint for lack of evidence because Garrett had already shipped the sculpture to its buyer.

FIGURE 3

Rapture

Candyce Garrett

Musical Recordings, Concerts Characterized as "Harmful to Minors"

Legislation is regularly proposed in states and localities around the country that would restrict the sale of concert tickets and recordings to minors based on the contention that certain of them are "harmful to minors." As these laws generally encompass a great deal of material that could not legally be kept from minors, their constitutionality is doubtful.

DEFAMATION

Defamation is the malicious harming of another's character or reputation by the publication of false facts either intentionally, negligently, or with reckless disregard for the truth. It includes both libel, which is written, and slander, which is spoken. Defamatory speech generally is not protected by the First Amendment. However, the First Amendment restricts the extent to which defamation laws can be used by public figures to punish speech on matters of public interest. Nor are expressions of opinion considered defamation. Specific legal tests govern the extent to which nonpublic figures and expression regarding matters not of public concern are legally actionable defamation.

FIGHTING WORDS

Expression that is designed and appears likely to provoke an immediate unlawful response from a specific and identifiable audience is not protected by the First Amendment. This is the famous "shouting 'fire' in a crowded theater" scenario, although the doctrine is much more narrow than those who frequently invoke it contend. To date, only spoken words have been considered "fighting words." The "fighting words" doctrine has not been applied to visual or literary arts.

Public Display Spaces

Government-owned public property is frequently the site of both formal and informal art exhibitions and performances. Galleries or theaters may be on land owned by the government or located in municipal buildings or public universities. Parks and plazas are often used for arts festivals and installations. Artists may choose to exhibit their works in parks or on public sidewalks.

Generally, the government cannot impose unreasonable or viewpoint-based restrictions on art in public spaces. The extent to which the government may place viewpoint-neutral restrictions that nevertheless discriminate against the subject matter of the art depends on whether the location of the exhibition or performance is considered a "public forum."

Public Forum

A public forum is public property that has been traditionally open to free expression or specially designated as a place for expression. Public property that fits neither of these categories is considered a nonpublic forum. Public forums are not limited to land or real property.

In a public forum, the government may not completely ban expression, but may enforce reasonable time, place, and manner restrictions. Time, place, and manner restrictions are exactly that: regulations on the time of expression, the specific placement of a presentation within a public area, and the manner in which the presentation is conducted. Restrictions on volume, the number of audience members, and the number of presenters are examples.

Time, place, and manner restrictions are permissible if they are reasonable and "content-neutral." A regulation is considered content-neutral as long as it serves a purpose unrelated to the content of the expression, even if enforcement of the regulation affects some messages but not others.

Reasonable time, place, and manner restrictions must leave open ample alternate channels for expression. Whether or not there are ample alternatives is a very specific determination that will vary for each situation. The key question is whether the speaker's ability to communicate effectively and reach the intended audience is threatened.

Time, place, and manner restrictions must also be *narrowly tailored* to serve a significant governmental objective. That is, the governmental objective would be achieved less effectively without the regulation. The restriction need not be the

Regulation of Communications Media

The broadcast communications media are regulated by the Federal Communications Commission. The government has greater ability to restrict the content of radio and broadcast television than other media. In 1978, the U.S. Supreme Court upheld the FCC's ruling that George Carlin's comedy routine, *Filthy Words*, although not legally obscene, could not be broadcast during certain times of the day. Television, which like radio "invades" the home and has historically been regulated by government, was also held to be subject to such restrictions. In 1997, the Supreme Court rejected requests to treat the Internet like radio and television, holding instead that the Internet enjoyed unqualified First Amendment protection like bookstores.

least restrictive means available for achieving the objective but must not be substantially broader than necessary. However, a restriction may be too broad if there are numerous and obvious less burdensome and more precise alternatives. In this respect, it is most relevant whether the regulation bans substantial expressive activity that does not contribute to the identified problem.

The government may place content-based restrictions on expression in a public forum only if the restriction is no greater than necessary to fulfill a compelling governmental interest. For example, a town could allow artists to paint images on the sidewalks but ban an artist from painting mock utility markings there because public health and safety concerns require that utility locations be clearly indicated.

A viewpoint-based restriction is presumed to be unconstitutional unless it can be shown that it is necessary to fulfill "a compelling governmental interest" and is the only method for achieving that goal. Therefore, the government cannot disallow the performance of a play that negatively portrays an elected official but allow plays that present a favorable portrayal.

Content-Based or Viewpoint-Based?

The distinction between content-based and viewpoint-based restrictions is not always easy to grasp. A viewpoint-based restriction is one that has as its rationale the specific motivating ideology or perspective of the speaker. A content-based restriction is one that affords differential treatment because of the subject matter, without regard for the stand taken with respect to the subject.

In 1991, a piece created by 18-year-old Jacob Roth for the 4-H exhibit at the Freeborn County (MN) Fair was removed only hours after it was installed. Roth intended the piece—which was composed of a mannequin dressed as Justice attached to a wooden cross with the sign "Women's Rights" above it—as a statement in support of abortion rights. Fair officials claimed the removal was content-based, that is, that "political statements" were not appropriate for the fair. However, an anti-abortion rights booth adorned with posters and models of aborted fetuses remained standing only a few feet from the 4-H exhibit. Roth eventually won an out-of-court settlement against the fair directors.

TRADITIONAL PUBLIC FORUMS

Traditional public forums are public areas that have been traditionally used for purposes of assembly, communication, and discussion such as parks, plazas, and sidewalks. These areas have been given this special constitutional protection in recognition of their historical role in and principal purpose of providing a place for the free exchange of ideas.

Street Artists and Performers Assert Right to Use Public Sidewalks

Public sidewalks have long been the location for a variety of artistic expression. Courts have generally upheld the rights of artists to use these areas for display, performance, or sale of art. In 1997, in a case brought by a group of artists who displayed and sold their art on city sidewalks, a federal appeals court ruled that New York City's General Vendors Law was unconstitutional. The law, which required nonfood vendors to apply for licenses to market their goods on public property, had been enforced against those who sold or displayed visual artworks, but not, in recognition of their free speech rights, against sellers of books, newspapers, and other written matter. New York street musicians recorded a similar victory when a judge ruled that a $45 fee the city charged for sound device permits was not adequately proportionate to the costs incurred by the city because of the street musicians. The measure was struck down as an inadequately tailored time, place, and manner restriction.

But street performers do not always enjoy unlimited use of public sidewalks. In 1993, Jessie Harris, a San Francisco comedian-magician performing under the name Casino, was sued by the owners of a Fisherman's Wharf shopping center who claimed that audience members obstructed the entrance to the center and hampered its tenants' ability to do business. A judge ruled that Harris could not perform on the public sidewalk immediately in front of the entrance to the shopping center while the center's shops accessible from that entrance were open for business.

DESIGNATED PUBLIC FORUMS

A designated public forum is public property that the government has intentionally made available for expression, even though the property has not traditionally had as its purpose the free exchange of ideas. However, an area is not considered a designated public forum merely because the government allows some speech activity there. For example, the U. S. Army does not open up the grounds of a military post to all musical performances because it allows the army marching band to perform there. Common examples of designated public forums might include a city hall art gallery or a theater in a public museum.

Some courts permit the government to dedicate a public space for a particular medium or subject matter, thereby creating a "limited" or "dedicated" public forum. Content-discrimination that preserves the purposes of a limited forum may be permissible. A city hall art gallery dedicated to artwork depicting landscapes may be permitted to exclude other subjects and may also ban live performance. A theater in a municipally owned children's museum may be permitted to limit performances to works intended for children. The limitations must be clearly defined and not merely left up to the unguided discretion of a governmental employee.

Other courts will consider these areas with substantial content restrictions to be nonpublic forums, as discussed below. A government may not, however, dedicate an area to the exhibition of a particular viewpoint unless the government itself is the exhibitor, or the restriction is necessary to further a very important governmental interest.

Community Room in Public Library Ruled a Limited Public Forum

The Community Room in the Manhasset (NY) Public Library is a space reserved for public uses that often include art exhibits. The library maintained an unwritten policy against the display of artwork depicting nudity. In 1993, Robyn Bellospirito, a local artist, applied to have her paintings displayed in the Community Room. Bellospirito's application was approved but she was not permitted to display three paintings that contained semi-nude females. Bellospirito sued the library claiming that her constitutional rights had been violated. The court agreed finding that the library had opened the Community Room for a multitude of speech-related uses, including the display of art, and was thus a dedicated public forum. The court held that the nudity prohibition was an insufficiently tailored, content-based restriction.

Nonpublic Forum

All other public property is considered a nonpublic forum. The government may ban expression altogether in a nonpublic forum—as long as the prohibition is reasonable—and may restrict expression that is not compatible with the forum's purpose.

Visual Artists Rights Act and Other Statutory Protection

The Visual Artists Rights Act (VARA), part of the federal copyright law, offers visual artists some legal protections against the modification of artwork and the removal of permanent installations. The act creates civil liability against those who intentionally distort, mutilate, or modify artwork in such a way that dishonors the artist. The law allows artists to prevent the intentional or grossly negligent destruction of work of "recognized stature." The law also protects the rights of artists to claim or disclaim authorship of artwork that has been modified or distorted. With respect to works that are part of a building that can be safely removed, the law requires the building owner to attempt to notify the artist and give the artist 90 days to remove the work. However, the law is fraught with exceptions and limitations, and the rights recognized under it may be waived by contract.

Several states also have laws protecting the integrity and attribution of visual artwork, including California, New York, Connecticut, Massachusetts, Pennsylvania, Rhode Island, Louisiana, Maine, New Jersey, and Nevada. These laws grant artists rights beyond those set out in VARA, including, in some cases, the provision of royalties on resale of artwork.

However, the restrictions cannot be unreasonable or an effort to suppress expression because of opposition to the speaker's viewpoint. A viewpoint-based restriction is illegal unless it is necessary to fulfill a compelling governmental interest. Thus, a mayor may prohibit all city employees from singing in a city hall conference room, but may not ban only the singing of songs that advocate an unpopular political position.

All Federal Buildings Not Necessarily Public Forums

The Public Buildings Cooperative Use Act, a 1976 law that directs administrators of public property to make appropriate spaces available for educational and cultural activities including art installations, apparently does not transform federal buildings into public forums. Artist Dayton Claudio, with the help of the American Civil Liberties Union (ACLU), sued the General Services Administration, the agency that administers federal buildings, after his permit to display *Sex, Laws and Coathangers* (Color Plate 1) in a federal building in Raleigh, North Carolina, was revoked in May 1992 because of the "political and controversial" nature of the work. The work depicts a nude female, fetus, and a coat hanger. A federal judge rejected Claudio's lawsuit, stating that the GSA was not required "to display a vulgar, shocking and tasteless painting" in the lobby of a federal building. The judge did not address the effect of the legislation in establishing the building as a public forum. A federal appellate court affirmed the judge's decision without comment.

Occasional Art Displays Do Not Transform Municipal Building into Public Forum

In 1996, a federal appeals court ruled that "limited expressive displays," such as occasional art exhibits, do not transform a governmental building into a public forum. The Austin (TX) Visual Arts Association was invited to submit artwork for display in the Austin municipal building. A piece by artist David Swim, *The Heart*, a lifecast of the torso of a nude male including genitalia (Fig. 4) was rejected by the city and the AVAA. The city cited concerns that the piece would disrupt the operation of the municipal building where city officials dealt with members of the general public. Swim was invited to submit a replacement piece, but declined and filed suit against the city. The trial court found that Swim's First Amendment rights were violated and awarded him damages for mental anguish. The appellate court reversed that decision, holding instead that the municipal building was not a public forum. The court drew a distinction between an area in which artists are invited to display art and an area, like the Austin building, where a sponsoring organization or an artist is merely invited to submit artwork for display. Public areas, the court noted, are considered public forums only to the extent the public is invited to use them. The court also found that the rejection of Swim's piece was not viewpoint discrimination because it was the effect of the display, and not the thought behind it, that was deemed inappropriate.

FIGURE 4
The Heart
David Swim

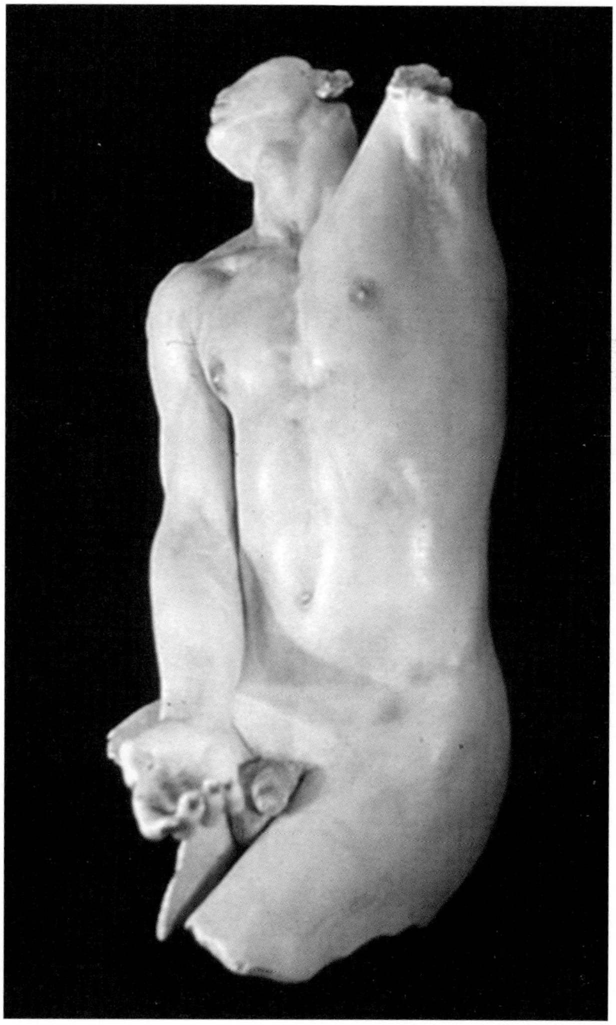

Government Funding and Sponsorship of the Arts

The government directly funds art in many ways—the National Endowment for the Arts; national, state, and local museums, symphonies, and theaters; and the Library of Congress are just a few examples. The government also indirectly supports arts by, for example, funding public universities, granting scholarships and student loans to art students, and granting tax and postal benefits to nonprofit arts organizations. The extent to which the government may legally restrict artistic expression that it funds is unclear. The more selective, competitive and subjective the funding process, the more control the government will likely maintain. Generally, it appears that whatever restrictions the government places on the use of its funds should be clearly enunciated and not left to the unfettered whim of officials.

Congress Directs NEA to Consider "Decency"

In 1989, controversy erupted over public funding for the arts. Elected officials accused the National Endowment for the Arts of funding "pornography" and "blasphemy" and attempted to eliminate the endowment, reduce its budget, and place restrictions on grant making. Sensitive to Congressional pressures, the NEA's National Council or chairperson made several funding decisions for political rather than artistic reasons. NCFE, along with the Center for Constitutional Rights and the ACLU, provided legal representation to four performance artists who filed a lawsuit after their grants were overturned by then NEA chair John Frohnmayer.

In 1990, Congress added language to the NEA's authorizing legislation that required that the agency in awarding grants consider "general standards of decency and respect for the diverse beliefs and values of the American public." The artists' lawsuit was then amended to challenge the constitutionality of this amendment and the National Association of Artists' Organizations was added to the lawsuit as another plaintiff.

FIGURE 5
Space Dance for Peace IV
Paul Goreniuc

The four artists settled their original claim against the NEA and received their original grant amounts plus damages. In June 1998, the Supreme Court upheld that the decency and respect standard finding that it merely added factors to the NEA's subjective and selective funding criteria and did not require the exclusion of any particular category of content. The Court cautioned the NEA against applying the standard so as to deny funding to works that expressed a particular viewpoint.

Similar scenarios continue to be played out at the state and local levels.

Governmental Regulation of Private Property

Government regulates the use of private lands through zoning laws. These laws may in some situations abridge free expression. Zoning laws generally do not violate the First Amendment if they are content-neutral time, place, and manner restrictions that serve a substantial governmental interest and do not unreasonably limit alternative avenues of communication.

Sometimes private property takes on so much of the character of public property that it is considered a public forum.

Expression in these areas may be limited as if these areas were public. The Supreme Court has recognized that a privately owned company town is subject to the same rules as a public town. Some states have recognized that shopping malls must treat sidewalks and hallways the same as public streets and sidewalks.

City Drops Attempt to Force Removal of Statue from Artist's Property

In 1997, sculptor Paul Goreniuc was served with a compliance order from the San Jose (CA) Department of Planning requiring him to remove his 12-foot-tall and 6-foot-wide sculpture *Space Dance for Peace IV* (Fig. 5) from the front yard of his home. The department claimed that Goreniuc was in violation of a local zoning ordinance that regulated the erection of "structures" on residential property. Following letters from NCFE and other national advocacy organizations, the city evaluated the situation and decided that the sculpture was not a "structure" within the meaning of the ordinance and dropped its action against Goreniuc.

Criminal Laws

The government may not criminalize expression protected by the First Amendment. But the types of expression discussed above that are not entitled to First Amendment protection are commonly criminalized. Most states have criminal laws regarding the distribution of obscene material or child pornography, and many state and local governments restrict the ways in which children are provided access to "adult" materials. Criminal laws, such as trespass laws, also may have the incidental effect of restricting expression. Laws such as these that, in combating criminal activity unrelated to artistic expression, indirectly limit artistic expression are valid as long as the law is reasonable and applied no more broadly than necessary to prevent the criminal conduct.

Other Laws

In some situations, laws that have other purposes may incidentally restrict artistic freedom. A law unrelated to the suppression of speech may be applied to restrict expression no more than is necessary to further the substantial governmental interest that underlies the law.

Sexual Harassment Laws

Many exhibition sites are also workplaces. While art museum employees may not find work with sexual content to be inappropriate for display, employees at a city hall—where the exhibition of art is not the primary purpose of the workplace—may be less tolerant. When art is displayed in a workplace, overly zealous interpretation of federal laws protecting employees from sexual harassment in the workplace may lead to the restriction of artistic content. The employer, which may be the government, may restrict content because it fears liability for sexual harassment. To what extent the freedom of artistic expression can legally be restricted by sexual harassment laws is still being examined in courts throughout the country.

In Murfreesboro, Tennessee, a painting by local artist Maxine Henderson entitled *Gwen* (Color Plate 2) was removed by city officials from an exhibition space in the city hall after a school board employee—who was at city hall to attend a job-related meeting—filed a sexual harassment complaint because of the painting. A judge ruled that Henderson's First Amendment rights had been violated because the city officials used unguided discretion in removing the painting. The judge did not rule on a new policy adopted after the incident, which specifically allows city officials to remove artwork they determine may expose the city to liability for sexual harassment.

Many other incidents have been resolved without a legal determination. An exhibit of woodcuts featuring nude figures by Zoravia Bettiol was removed from the Menlo Park (CA) City Hall in March 1993 following a sexual harassment complaint by a city worker. The exhibit was reinstalled two years later as part of the settlement of a lawsuit brought by the artist.

A planned exhibit of pen and pencil drawings by Carmen Trujillo, scheduled for display at CIA headquarters, was canceled because some of the drawings depicted silhouetted female breasts. The CIA cited concerns about sexual harassment. Three of Trujillo's drawings were confiscated and ultimately lost by the CIA.

Marc Simmons's painting of his daughter and her friends sitting on the beach (Color Plate 3) was removed from the Workers Compensation Commission offices in Hartford, Connecticut, because of fears that it would provoke a sexual harassment complaint.

A mural in the post office in Oglesby, Illinois, became the subject of a sexual harassment complaint 51 years after it was installed by Chicago artist Fay Davis. The mural, which depicted 14 Native Americans in loin cloths, some with bare buttocks exposed and leaves adhering to their genitalia, was covered by blinds while the complaint was pending.

Citing a newly created sexual harassment law that forbids the display of sexually explicit, embarrassing, or demeaning materials in offices or public restrooms, city officials in Auburn, Washington, refused to allow weaver Inge Norgaard to include three of her tapestries in a show being hung at the Auburn City Hall. The tapestries were based on Norse mythology and depicted a nursing mother, a nude woman carrying a torch, and a nude male.

Sexual harassment laws were also cited in attacks against the Spokane (WA) City Hall exhibition of Cecilia Alvarez's painting depicting a poisoned Mother Earth giving birth to Death (Color Plate 4). Alvarez's piece remained on display after the mayor viewed it and found it "quite beautiful."

Religious Art on Public Lands

The First Amendment also prohibits the establishment or endorsement by the government of a particular religious belief. When the government opens its property as a public forum or creates a general funding program for private expression it may not discriminate against religious perspectives. Nevertheless. public art presentations with strong religious content may draw accusations that the government is endorsing a particular religion.

The Arts Council of Fairfax County (VA), which coordinates the placement of art in public buildings throughout the county, adopted a policy in 1989 that prohibited religious imagery, along with several other categories of images, from any art displayed in public. As a result, Edgar Boshart's photograph of the San Francisco de Asis Church and Esta Gladstone's photograph of a 92-year-old Jewish man praying were removed from a 1994 exhibit in a county building. After an exchange of letters with the ACLU and the American Jewish Congress, the Arts Council dropped its policy.

COLOR PLATE 1
Sex, Laws, and Coathangers
Dayton Claudio

COLOR PLATE 2
Gwen
Maxine Henderson

COLOR PLATE 3
Girls on the Beach
Marc Simmons

FIGURE 6
Stand Up and Speak Out
Mike Alfano

Due Process

The Constitution guarantees criminal defendants the right to due process of law. Mike Alfano's sculpture *Stand Up and Speak Out* (Fig. 6) was removed from in front of the Nassau (NY) County Courthouse after defense attorneys complained that the artwork could prejudice jurors against drunk driving defendants, in violation of those defendants' due process rights. The sculpture depicted two persons coming to the aid of a drunk driving victim. The sculpture was relocated to the county medical center.

Types of Art Most Frequently Challenged

Challenges to artistic freedom are most frequently based on viewpoint or subject matter. Nudity and sexuality, religion, race, violence, and politics are the most common flash points. As can be seen from the examples below, it is often difficult to anticipate what type of art will rouse someone's ire enough to cause her or him to publicly protest its display.

FIGURE 7
The Reclining Bacchante
Jim Bostick

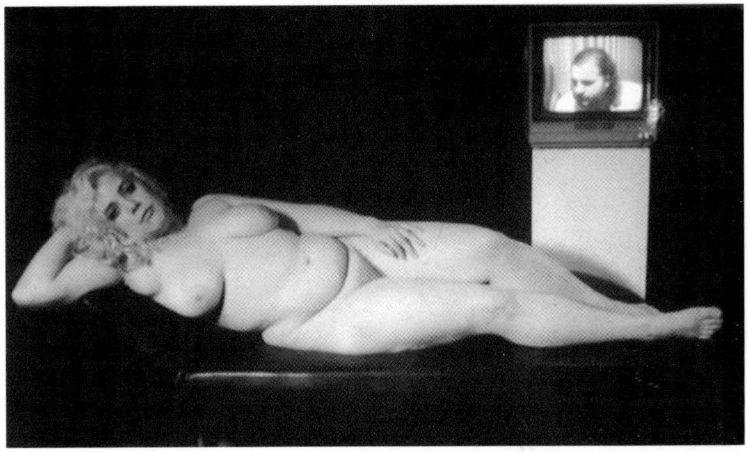

Sexual Content

Sexual content is perhaps the most common source of controversy. Art depicting nudity or addressing sexuality is challenged as being inappropriate for minors and being morally corrupt in and of itself. Critics often do not distinguish between graphic anatomical depictions and stylized, nonexplicit representations of the human form. Nor do they distinguish between nudity and eroticism. Male nudity, particularly erect penises, is targeted disproportionately to female nudity. Homosexuality can also be a bright red flag. Depictions of women in submissive, exploitative, or violent sexual situations have been targeted by some women's rights organizations that equate such images to "fighting words." Images interpreted as masturbation remain largely taboo. As discussed earlier, art incorporating images of nude or provocatively posed minors or implying minors in sexual situations is frequently challenged as child pornography.

FIGURE 8
Joshua in Repose
Steve Johnson

Nudity

Jim Bostick's photograph *The Reclining Bacchante* (Fig. 7) was removed from a juried show at the Marietta (PA) Restoration Association shortly after it was judged "Best of Show" because it was deemed "out of character with the spirit of the exhibit." Steve Johnson's *Joshua in Repose* (Fig. 8) was also removed, even though the subject's genitals were not visible. Exhibit officials dismissed the judges and rejudged the show themselves. An apology was issued after

COLOR PLATE 4
Modern Living Through Chemistry
Cecilia Alvarez

COLOR PLATE 5
The Philly Flasher
Emerson Zabower

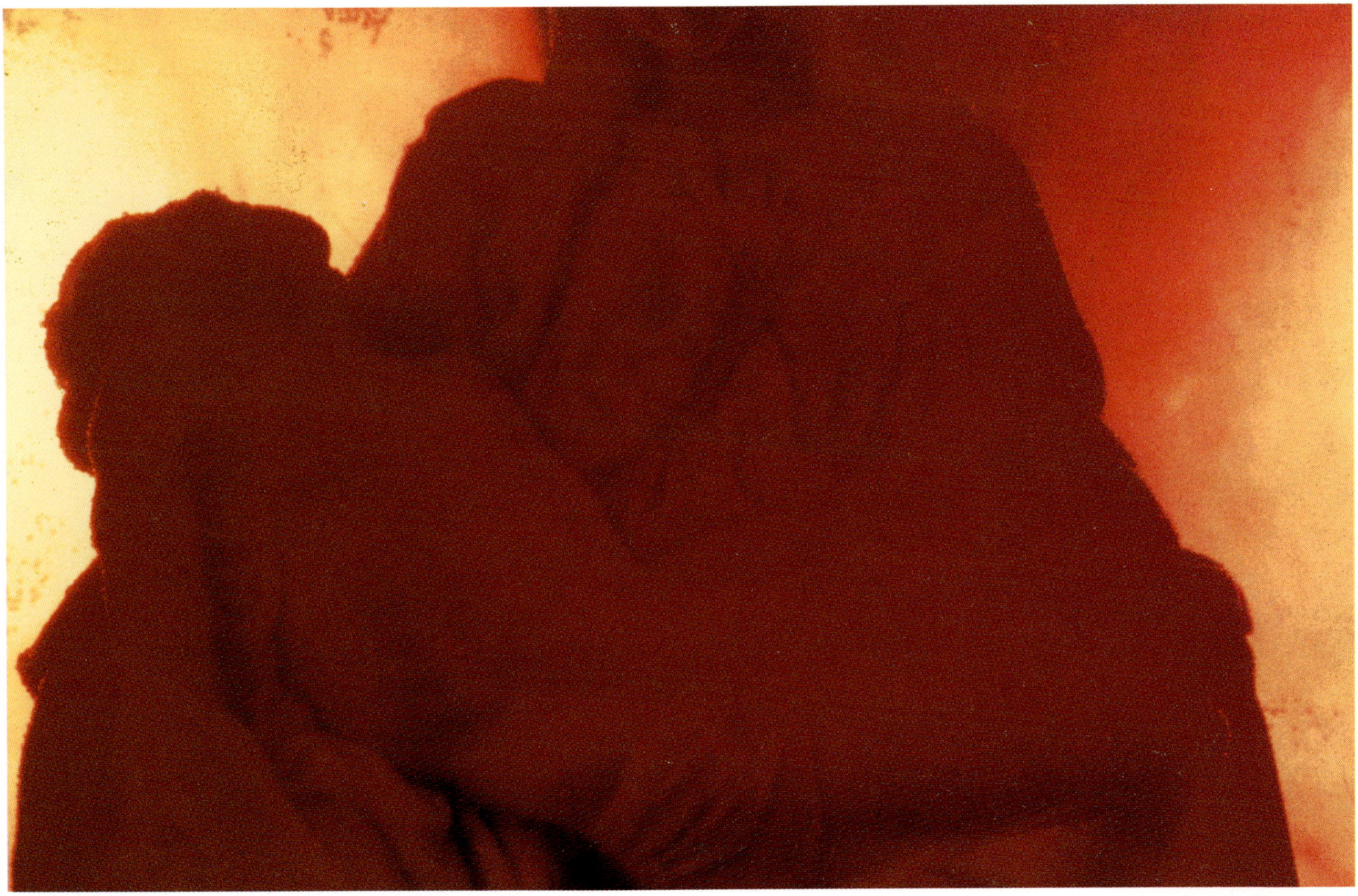

COLOR PLATE 6
Pieta II
Andres Serrano

FIGURE 9
To the Democrats, Republicans, and Bipartisans
Sharon Rupp

FIGURE 10
In Awe
Janette Hopper

litigation was brought. Sharon Rupp's *To the Democrats, Republicans, and Bipartisans* (Fig. 9) and ten of Janette Hopper's linoleum prints, including *In Awe* (Fig. 10), were excluded from an exhibition at the Pasco (WA) City Hall because they depicted simple, nonsexual nudity. City officials characterized the works as "sexually suggestive," "prurient," and "pornographic."

Male Nudity

Seattle photographer Patrice Ridenour submitted three photographs for an exhibit at the Grace Cultural Center in Abilene, Texas. Two photographs that depicted male frontal nudity were excluded, while the third, which depicted female frontal nudity, was not. The show was ultimately canceled by the organizers to protest the double standard. In 1997, *The Philly Flasher* (Color Plate 5), by Emerson Zabower was relocated from the main exhibit area at the Johnson City (TN) Arts Council to the director's office after an arts council volunteer protested its display. Other of Zabower's paintings in the same exhibit featuring female nudity were not objected to. Performances of John Guare's award-winning play *Six Degrees of Separation* have been challenged several times because of the brief on-stage presence of a naked man.

Homosexuality

Officials in Cobb County, Georgia, eliminated all county arts funding rather than fund work they believed promoted a "gay agenda." County commissioners were upset by productions of David Henry Hwang's *M. Butterfly* and Terrence McNally's *Lips Together, Teeth Apart*. The latter includes references to gay men, but has no gay characters. In early 1996, a group of Washington state legislators demanded the removal from the state capitol of an exhibit of photographs depicting gays, lesbians, and bisexuals in their communities and workplaces. The exhibit, entitled *Family, Friends and Neighbors*, (Fig 11, 12, 13) had no sexual content. The state declined to remove the exhibit.

FIGURES 11-13
from Family, Friends & Neighbors
Jim Folts

COLOR PLATE 8
Letters Home III
Mona Waterhouse

COLOR PLATE 7
Initiation
Donnell

COLOR PLATE 9
Artist Richard Taylor painting original mural image

COLOR PLATE 10
Richard Taylor's Proposed Image for Venice Graffiti Pit

Religious or Anti-Religious Content

Art with religious themes or imagery, or anything that might be interpreted as such, is also frequently challenged. Challenges are leveled at works interpreted as demeaning a particular religious belief as well as those interpreted as promoting atheism, paganism, or Satanism.

Blasphemy and Sacrilege

Student groups at the University of Alabama at Birmingham protested the university's acquisition of photographer Andres Serrano's *Pieta II* (Color Plate 6). The photograph shows the image of Michelangelo's statue of Jesus and the Virgin Mary submerged in urine. The student council passed a resolution calling the purchase "frivolous" and "offensive." An exhibit of paintings by Houston artist Donnell (Color Plate 7) was closed abruptly after protests from local Catholic groups, including the Archdiocese of San Antonio. The exhibit, *Spiritual, Sensual, Sexual,* was originally displayed in a gallery space on the grounds of a San Antonio retirement center for nuns. The nuns had approved the show prior to its installation. Critics claimed the exhibit "damaged the good name of the Catholic Church."

"I know better now not to send my work to Alabama."
Mona Waterhouse, *artist*

Witchcraft

The University of Mobile (AL) removed a painting by Mona Waterhouse after viewers complained that the piece contained "demonic symbols." *Letters Home III* (Color Plate 8) depicted runes and rune stone symbols that told a story of the artist's Swedish heritage, family, and friends. The university president told Waterhouse that the painting was removed so that the community would not think she was a witch. Members of the Evangelical Free Church in Rockwell City, Iowa, convinced the local school superintendent to cancel a performance by storyteller Nancy Duncan. The church claimed that Duncan promoted witchcraft and the occult in telling the Russian folktale of Baba Yaga, a 600-year-old witch. Several other of Duncan's engagements were either threatened or canceled following protests by an organized network of religious groups throughout the Midwest.

Violence

Art about or including physical violence is frequently challenged. The primary claim by critics is that violent descriptions or depictions cause violent behavior in children and certain adults; a claim that is not borne out by scientific research. Legal challenges have focused on violence as being "fighting words," but courts have not found that artistic renderings of violence are likely or designed to cause imminent unlawful conduct.

Images and descriptions of gang violence and what critics perceive to be anti–law enforcement sentiment have drawn particularly zealous challenges, as expected, from the law enforcement community. Certain women's rights organizations and activists commonly challenge depictions of rape and other violent acts against women, including violent sexual imagery. Challenges to violent content have arisen with respect to each arts medium.

FIGURE 14
Graffiti on the building next to the Round Valley Inn
Marian Azbill

Gangs and Criticisms of Law Enforcement

In November 1996, a panel of four photographs by local resident Marian Azbill (Fig. 14), including an image of a graffito reading "cop killer," was removed from an exhibit in the Mendocino County (CA) Administration Center at the request of the county sheriff. The panel was ordered reinstalled a week later by the chair of the board of supervisors after protests from arts and civil liberties groups. A mural depicting a graffiti artist being clubbed by a pig in a blue suit (Color Plate 9) was ordered removed from the Venice Graffiti Pit by the Los Angeles Recreation and Parks Commission because of what it felt was an anti–law enforcement message. Officials also rejected a proposed replacement image depicting a large pig looming over a family fleeing down an urban street (Color Plate 10). The Rockford (IL) School District

COLOR PLATE 11

What Is the Proper Way to Display the U.S. Flag?

Dread Scott

COLOR PLATE 12
Our Lady of Pysanky
Ellen Zahorec

removed *Always Running* by Luis J. Rodriguez from school library shelves because school board members found the story of Rodriguez's experiences as a gang member in Los Angeles "harmful, ungodly and wrong," "irreligious, anti-family, left-wing, anti-American, and radical."

In 1998, rap musician C-BO was jailed following the release of his album *Til My Casket Drops*. California corrections officials claimed that the distribution of the recording violated a condition of the artist's parole that prevented him from recording music that "promotes gang violence" or was "anti–law enforcement." C-BO unsuccessfully tried to have the condition removed from his parole record three times before releasing the recording. The specific charge of a violation based on that recording was ultimately dropped, but the condition remained in place.

Violence Against Women and Violent Sexual Imagery

The owner and manager of The Newsstand in Bellingham, Washington, were acquitted on obscenity charges stemming from their sale of *Answer Me*, a magazine published by Jim and Debbie Goad. The magazine depicted rape, sexual torture, and murder using graphic language, drawings, and photographs. The prosecution arose from a complaint filed by the director of a local crisis center. In 1997, the National Organization of Women and other prominent feminist groups protested the sale of the song *Smack My Bitch Up* by the musical group Prodigy. The song's entire lyrics are "Change my pitch up/Smack my bitch up." In response to protests, major retailers Wal-Mart and Kmart pulled the album that included the song from their shelves. The video to the song, which depicted a young man using drugs, vomiting, grabbing women, having sex with a stripper, and fighting, was also subject to numerous protests.

Television Violence

Complaints regarding the "violent" content of television programming have led to several legislative efforts to control the content of that medium. Chief among them is the V-chip, named for its purported ability to block out programming with violent, sexual, or other "objectionable,"content. The law mandates that the V-chip be installed on all new television sets and that the FCC "prescribe"a ratings system to coordinate with the V-chip if the industry does not do so "voluntarily."

Race and Ethnicity

Concerns regarding racial and ethnic equality or sensitivity drive many challenges to artistic freedom. Some artistic expression about race is stigmatized as "hate speech" or "politically incorrect" in the same way that some expression about sex is tagged "pornography." These challenges can place civil liberties organizations in a bind between their constituents who believe that such expression does great damage to hard-won civil rights gains and those who believe that such expression must be tolerated and defended. Often the message is simply misunderstood.

Race

A painting by Chicago artist David Nelson depicting the recently deceased Mayor Harold Washington in women's underwear was removed from the main corridor of the Chicago Art Institute only hours after it was installed. The supposed racism of the painting was the subject of wide-scale protests. Books that use racially derogatory language, such as Mark Twain's *The Adventures of Huckleberry Finn* and Richard Wright's *Black Boy* and *Native Son*, face very frequent challenges to their places on library shelves and in school curricula.

Ethnicity

In 1984, Congressman Mario Biaggi (D-NY) criticized the National Endowment for the Arts for supporting a production of Verdi's *Rigoletto* by the Metropolitan Opera and the Virginia Opera Company. The production depicted several characters as members of the Mafia. Biaggi considered the production to be disparaging of Italian-Americans and proposed amending the NEA statute to prohibit the use of funds in "any manner to denigrate any ethnic, racial, religious, or minority group." The amendment failed.

A planned broadcast by a public television station in New York of the BBC production of Shakespeare's *The Merchant of Venice* brought protests from several prominent Jewish organizations including the Anti-Defamation League, and the Committee to Bring Nazi War Criminals to Justice. The play has also been removed from libraries and classrooms because of complaints that it is anti-Semitic.

Political Content

Art with political content is subject to attack by those who disagree with the political views expressed in the work as well as those who believe that any political content is inappropriate in art. The belief that public monies should not be spent on political activity has led to challenges to government support of artwork with strong political content. A wide range of topics, for example, abortion, communism, political parties and figures, the environment, and war, may incite challenges.

Art Demonized as "Propaganda"

In September 1997, The Esperanza Center, a San Antonio organization that combines arts programming and social justice advocacy, was stripped of its city arts funding by the city council. Council members cited Esperanza's "in your face" leftist political programming as the main reason for the defunding. In 1993, a traveling exhibit of paintings by North Vietnamese artists about the Vietnam War was canceled by museum directors in Minneapolis and San Jose, California. Objectors, including some South Vietnamese immigrants, characterized the exhibit as "propaganda."

Cuban Art and Artists

Anti-Castro sentiment is an ongoing motivation for challenges to even nonpolitical arts and cultural programs. In 1996, the Dade County (FL) Center for the Fine Arts canceled a visit by Cuban scholar and art critic Gerardo Mosquera for fear of alienating the community. The cancellation followed a concert by Cuban pianist Gonzalo Rubacala at which 200 protesters verbally and physically assaulted audience members. In 1997, a Dade County Film, Television, and Print Advisory Board member was removed from her position after merely suggesting that the county reconsider its policy of excluding Cuban artists from its music festival. In June 1996, a Massachusetts principal requested that a third grade student alter his drawing that was part of a mural addressing the question "What is respect?" The drawing featured the Cuban and American flags with the words "Showdown between Clinton and Castro." The principal, who was eventually convinced to allow the images to remain, considered the images to be "unpatriotic" and "negative."

Patriotism

Art that addresses issues of American heritage is commonly challenged as unpatriotic or as an affront to veterans. The most frequent examples of these challenges are those aimed at work that incorporates imagery of the American flag. The Supreme Court has held that physical desecration of the flag, of which some artists using flags or flag imagery have been accused, is constitutionally protected expression. However, a constitutional amendment that would allow states to criminalize flag desecration is regularly put forward. Resulting legislation could well prohibit artistic uses of the flag.

Members of Congress Challenge Flag Art

A nationwide protest erupted around *Old Glory: The American Flag in Contemporary Art*, an exhibit at the Phoenix Art Museum in the spring of 1996. The show included Dread Scott's *What Is the Proper Way to Display the U.S. Flag?* (Color Plate 11), which consisted of a flag draped on the ground surmounted by a comment book that could only be accessed by walking on the flag. Congressional leaders and other protesters called for the exhibit's closing. The museum stood firmly for freedom of expression and kept the exhibit on display and unedited during its scheduled run despite the fact that at least one funder withdrew support and others threatened to do the same. In an earlier incident in Chicago, a court found that Dread Scott's piece was protected expression.

U.S. representative Peter King (R-NY) claimed that Donald Lipski's *Flag Ball No. 3* "offended good taste, decency, and reverence for the American flag" while it was on display on the campus of Long Island University. Vandals later destroyed the piece (Cover).

FIGURE 15
Hidden Heart
Scott Church

Based on Name Only

It is not unusual for artwork to be attacked based solely on its name with little reference to the content of the work and regardless of whether the title itself contains profanity. In Annville, Pennsylvania, organizers were forced to cancel a multimedia exhibit when concerns arose in the local community about the exhibition's title: *Sex Is Art*

(Fig. 15). A local official, while admitting that he had not seen any of the works to be included in the exhibit, declared that "our community standards don't accept this filth." Artist Ellen Zahorec canceled the multi-artist show—*Immaculate Misconceptions* (Color Plate 12)—she had coordinated for exhibition at Northern Kentucky University's Main Gallery, after a storm of controversy erupted over the "blasphemous" title. Gallery officials in Boston accepted Jerry Hooten's linoleum print *Wishbone* (Fig. 16)—depicting a shirtless male affectionately carrying another shirtless male on his back—for inclusion in an exhibit celebrating gay and lesbian pride on the condition that Hooten come up with a less suggestive title. Hooten declined.

FIGURE 16
Wishbone
Jerry Hooten

Or For Any Reason

Sometimes it is truly difficult to anticipate what is going to offend a reader, a viewer, or an audience member. In 1996, two works by photographer Beth Wesson (Fig. 17) were rejected for a planned exhibit at the Midtown YMCA Photo Gallery in New York because they were deemed "too disturbing and too frightening" for children and mentally ill individuals who might pass by the exhibit. Education officials in California took exception to Alice Walker's story *Am I Blue?* because they considered it "anti–meat eating" and moved to remove an excerpt of it from a tenth grade standardized test. They relented following pressure from free speech advocates. In 1997, a California legislator, with the endorsement of Vice President Gore, called for public hearings to educate the film industry about the consequences of depicting tobacco use in movies. Proponents of the measure claimed that such depictions caused young children to start smoking.

FIGURE 17
Untitled
Beth Wesson

Preparing for, Understanding, and Responding to Challenges to Your Freedom of Artistic Expression

In the controversies that engulfed the arts community in the 1980s and 1990s, artists, arts organizations, and arts supporters expended great energies and resources reacting to crises.

In this defensive posture, the arts community had little time and few resources for proactive advocacy. Actively advocating for artistic freedom, even in the absence of a specific challenge, nurtures a strong and supportive arts community that honors and appreciates free expression. By being proactive, you can create a climate of greater tolerance and understanding in which challenges are less likely to occur. By organizing your arts community and fostering informed dialogue on the issues in the general community, you can help ensure that when challenges do occur, the issues are discussed in an intelligent manner.

And a proactive approach allows for challenges to be responded to with greater efficiency and effectiveness. Indeed, the value of advance planning cannot be overstated.

Mobilize Your Community Before a Challenge

Actively promoting freedom of artistic expression need not be a solitary endeavor. All facets of your local arts community should share artistic freedom as a common goal. By organizing and mobilizing your community, you can more effectively advocate a variety of issues of common interest and become a powerful and influential presence in the greater community, even in the absence of a specific challenge.

Form a Local Freedom of Expression Organization

Local arts communities can empower themselves by forming local arts advocacy and free expression groups. Organizations of this type can actively promote artistic freedom and free speech in general by holding symposia and panel discussions and sponsoring performances or exhibits that present artistic freedom issues in an intelligent and persuasive manner. These groups can also act as a unified voice of the arts community by speaking out on issues of public concern.

By forming local anti-censorship organizations, communities also can help prevent challenges and respond effectively when artists or organizations are challenged. Free expression organizations can educate and mobilize the community, supply knowledgeable and favorable media contacts, and provide moral support to individuals being challenged. Such organizations can plan educational events in advance of the opening of a potentially controversial exhibit or performance to raise community awareness about the principles of artistic freedom. A free expression group can also monitor local, state, and national legislation that threatens First Amendment rights.

Local free expression groups can also act as a liaison between your local community and national advocacy organizations such as NCFE. NCFE regularly corresponds with several local groups that keep us up to date on incidents in and near their communities. And NCFE looks to local organizations to assist in addressing challenges that may have an impact on their areas.

Look within and beyond the arts community when forming these networks. Consider the range of individuals and organizations that have an interest in freedom of expression: librarians, booksellers, audience members, performing arts sponsors, journalists, galleries, video store owners, record merchandisers, university faculty, labor unions, members of the clergy, and so on. Determine whether any local public officials or members of the press support your position. Investigate whether any existing local organizations are involved in freedom of expression. Don't ever assume that anyone is an ally or an enemy. You may be surprised who your strongest supporters are.

Some national religious organizations, such as the Interfaith Alliance, Baptist Joint Convention, National Council on Churches, and B'nai Brith, follow free speech issues and may have a local office.

NCFE and some of the other national organizations listed in Appendix II can assist you in forming a local free expression group.

Adopt a Statement of Artistic Freedom Principles

Members of a local arts community may also find it useful to adopt a Statement of Artistic Freedom Principles. A statement of this type is an informal understanding among artists, presenters, and audience and community members that acknowledges the importance of freedom of artistic expression and respect for the ability to decide for oneself what art one will or will not experience. The statement can serve as an agreement that presenters or audience members will not assert censorial pressures on an artist because of the content of artwork, even if the work becomes subject to controversy or is personally offensive. Support for such a statement by a cross-section of the community is a powerful tool to present to local officials who must make decisions regarding the use of public spaces for exhibitions and performances.

The statement can also delineate a procedure explaining how a presenter will respond to complaints against presented art. Such procedures can be of varying detail but should ensure that the artist is kept apprised of the complaints and involved in the decision regarding whether to modify the presentation. Many communities find it useful to require complaints to be submitted in writing and to set up formal procedures for hearing all sides of a challenge.

Sample Statements of Artistic Freedom Principles are included Appendix III.

Cultivate Good Relationships with the Media and Elected Officials

You will have an advantage and be more credible when your art is challenged if you have a pre-existing relationship with the media and with your local elected officials. Invite them to forums or to board meetings for discussions. Provide opportunities for them to speak and ask questions. And after favorable treatment, thank-you notes and cards are always appreciated and remembered.

Know Your Opposition

Educate yourself and your community about individuals and groups—local and national—most likely to challenge artistic freedom. Become familiar with the major players, their motivations, and their tactics. The more you can involve your opposition in discussions regarding artistic freedom before an incident, the more likely the debate surrounding the incident will be conducted in a civil and intelligent manner.

Preparing for a Specific Potential Challenge

By anticipating challenges and preparing materials and programs in advance of likely controversial presentations, you can transform a potentially contentious situation into a beneficial one.

Challenges can often be avoided if those who might be offended by the artwork understand the artist's concept and reasons for creating the work. Prepare educational materials to accompany the presentation, and host discussions or lectures regarding the controversial issues. Offer the artist a chance to explain the work and address potential complaints. Allow a forum for comments to be made. Many challenges arise when the critic of the work has no other opportunity to speak out about the piece.

Prepare the greater community for the presentation by discussing the content with them prior to opening, and solicit from them what materials they desire to properly understand the presentation. By working together like this, you can establish long-term relationships based on mutual trust that may head off challenges in the future.

Gallery Works with Greater Community in Advance of Klan Exhibit

The Southeastern Center for Contemporary Art (SECCA) in Winston-Salem, North Carolina, realized that its upcoming exhibit, *Reconstruction: William Christenberry's Art,* posed potential problems with members of the public because of its inclusion of Ku Klux Klan–related art. SECCA feared that members of the community might take the work out of context and interpret it as racist and as an endorsement of the Klan. Working with Christenberry, SECCA set out to ensure that people understood Christenberry's intent to document, not politicize the subject matter, an intent SECCA feared might not be obvious when merely viewing the exhibit. Prior to the exhibit's opening, SECCA invited members of the local community of all races to discuss the exhibit and the issues it raised. SECCA organized eight roundtable discussions moderated by a professional facilitator, soliciting ideas and recommendations for ensuring that the exhibit would prove constructive to the community. The center worked with the local arts council to recruit a local expert on African-American culture to speak at the gallery, and previewed the exhibit for community leaders, asking for suggestions and recommendations.

In response to the feedback, SECCA embarked on an ambitious but effective course. The center developed a resource area with materials regarding racism and intolerance. SECCA implemented a tour policy that provided only limited access to the Klan portion of the exhibit to students in grades below the eighth grade. The center also provided materials to teachers and asked them to preview the exhibit before bringing classes there. An audio tape of Christenberry explained his background and his interest in Klan art, and film and video presentations and speakers addressed race relations during the run of the exhibit.

The show ran successfully with almost no incidents or complaints.

CHAPTER 3

Responding to

Understanding, Preparing for, and Responding to Challenges to Your Freedom of Artistic Expression

Freedom of speech in general, and artistic freedom in particular, are integral components of a free democratic society. It is a fundamental constitutional principle that our society benefits from the free exchange of ideas and that each individual has the right and ability to decide for him or herself what to hear, see, speak, sing, paint, sculpt, dance, and perform. Standing up against one challenge may discourage future challenges and discourage other artists from self-censoring. Resisting a challenge can validate the work or works at issue by stimulating informed discussion.

However, fighting back against challenges to your freedom of artistic expression can be physically, emotionally, and financially draining. It can place a tremendous burden on you or your staff. It can also adversely affect your relationship with presenters, funders, neighbors, and colleagues. Although some challenges are resolved in a few days, others may drag on for years.

Organizations such as NCFE can alleviate some of the burden. We have learned a lot since 1990 and this Handbook is the result.

This section is directed at both individual artists and organizations (arts and others) presenting an exhibit, performance, screening, or reading that is challenged. Some of the items described below are more pertinent to organizations, but individuals can benefit from them as well.

Get the Facts

The first step in fighting challenges to artistic freedom is to identify and record all of the relevant facts about the challenge. A thorough but concise outline of the facts will help you in writing letters, developing media statements, discussing your situation with attorneys, and informing your public and your funders.

- Identify precisely the work being challenged. Is it an entire exhibit, one piece, or merely a single element or theme within a piece? Is it an entire performance, a single song, or one lyric within a song?

- Identify those challenging your artistic freedom. It is critical in developing an effective defense to properly identify the individuals and organizations mounting the challenge. If you have been ordered to remove, modify, or cancel a performance or exhibition, identify the person and/or entity that had authority to order that action as well as any persons or entities that effectively encouraged that action.

- Identify the reason for the challenge. Find out what offended the challenger and what the stated justification is for the challenge. These are not always the same.

- Identify the site of the presentation. Your legal protections may vary significantly according to the location of the performance or exhibition. The location may also influence your non-legal response strategy.

- Create a comprehensive timeline of all key events and all key decisions. When was the first complaint made? When did the arts council meet? When was the sculpture removed? When did a criminal investigation begin? When are grants distributed?

- Identify key decision makers. If you have not yet been ordered to remove, cancel, or modify a performance or exhibit, find out who would be in charge of making that decision. For example, your opposition may be a single member of the city council backed up by a citizens' group. However, the decision to cancel your performance may lie with the remaining council members or the mayor.

- Identify avenues of appeal. In many cases, it is possible to have a "final" decision reconsidered. Determine if there are any legislative or administrative appeal procedures. Exhibition contracts may set out specific appeal processes.

- Determine your desired resolution. What do you want to happen? Do you want to have your photograph rehung? An adequate, alternative performance space found? An apology issued? Compensation for monetary damages? An open forum held on the issue?

Set out all this information in a simple fact sheet. Include all important contact numbers. You may want to have slightly different versions—one for the media, another for board members, and so on. A sample fact sheet is included in Appendix III.

Notify Involved Parties

Distribute your fact sheet to staff, board members, funders, the artists involved, other affected artists, and members and subscribers. Meet with staff and explain the situation. Designate one person who will handle outside inquiries regarding the challenge.

Enlist Key Allies

Contact Advocacy and Service Organizations

Contact a national free speech organization such as NCFE, your local ACLU affiliate, People for the American Way, or the National Coalition Against Censorship. If a local free speech group exists, contact it.

Look also to your local and state arts advocacy organizations. However, be aware that some may be reluctant to choose sides in local controversies. Present your situation to them, and emphasize its impact on broad cultural policy. Determine if any local university art, literature, theater, or media department can offer you resources or support.

There are also national service organizations for particular media or demographics, such as the College Art Association, the Society for Photographic Education, and National Association of Latino Arts and Culture.

See Appendix II for a list of national advocacy and service organizations.

Identify Allies within Your Community

As discussed above, cast a big net in identifying allies in your community. Look to journalists, librarians, booksellers, academics, members of the clergy, arts patrons, as well as representatives from all arts disciplines. National organizations may be able to mobilize their supporters locally in your defense. Most of the national service organizations have members in every state. If you have a local freedom of expression group, much of this work may already have been done for you.

Determine whether any public officials or prominent members of your community support your position. And do not forget the people who come to your performances and exhibitions. They may be your most persuasive advocates.

Mobilize Community Support

Contact Your Local Supporters

In many incidents you will need to contact your allies frequently to keep them abreast of developments, hearings, rallies, and so on. A telephone/fax/email tree will help you disseminate information rapidly. The coordinator activates the "tree" by calling the first tier of supporters. Each supporter on the first tier then contacts several members of the second tier and so on.

Action alerts can be an effective means to organize phone and letter-writing campaigns and other grassroots activities. An action alert should be brief, providing essential background information, and outlining the specific steps you are asking allies to take. It is helpful to provide sample letters or phone scripts, but you should also emphasize that personalized communications are generally more effective. Action alerts can be distributed via fax, email, phone tree, organizational newsletter, or postings at galleries, performance spaces, coffee shops, or bookstores. A sample action alert is included in Appendix III.

Start a Letter Writting Campaign

Ask supporters to write letters on behalf of your position. Letters should be directed to the challengers, the decision makers, local newspapers, and governmental officials. It is helpful for a wide variety of your local and national allies to write letters on your behalf. Sample letters are included in Appendix III.

Letters and faxes are preferred because they provide decision makers with a written record of support for your position. However, when time is short, consider telephone calls, email, or distributing postcards to your allies with a preprinted message for immediate mailing.

Organize Public Discussion

Challenges to freedom of artistic expression are excellent opportunities for educating the community about freedom of expression or the specific subject matter that has raised the challenge. Public discourse and dialogue can transform even the most contentious challenges into constructive discussions.

Produce a symposium, forum, or panel discussion about artistic freedom. Consider inviting those on both sides of the issue, and present a balanced, intelligent account. Providing the artists, curators, or directors the opportunity to speak directly about their work is almost always a good idea. It is also helpful to include a panelist who is familiar with the broader incidence of censorship and can contextualize the incident at hand.

Stage a Public Demonstration

Consider staging a public demonstration in support of your position. This can be a rally, parade, or picket. These events are more appropriate for incidents of longer duration rather than for those likely to resolve themselves in a few days. Organizing a public demonstration is very time consuming but it can be effective in demonstrating community support and attracting media attention to your position. However, a poorly attended rally or one that proves disproportionately disruptive can harm your cause. As always, be careful not to demonize or personally attack your opposition. Instead focus on promoting your values of freedom, liberty, and democracy.

Confront the Challengers

Make sure those challenging your work, and those who will make any decisions about whether your work will appear, know that you are aware of your rights and are going to defend your work zealously. As always, resist the temptation to respond to challenges on a purely emotional level or by vilifying your critics. Don't belittle your opposition or their beliefs. The most effective letters, discussions, and presentations are those that acknowledge your opposition's concerns but present your position intelligently and rationally.

- Write to the decision makers to defend your work and the principles of freedom of expression. Inform the decision makers that you are aware of your constitutional rights—they might not be—and that you will resist their efforts. Be brief and direct. A sample protest letter is included in Appendix III.

- Make every effort to attend the decision-making sessions. Bring supporters along, and ask respected community members to speak on your behalf. Ask to make a presentation in defense of the art. Be concise, clear, and informed. When the government is involved, you will most likely have a right to attend a meeting and be heard.

Presentation at Public Hearing Saves Funding

From 1992 to 1997, Out North Contemporary Art House in Anchorage, Alaska, survived five attempts to eliminate large public grants. Out North has not relied on a single strategy to preserve its funding but has tried to match its response to the specifics of each challenge. It has defended itself in court, before funding panels, and to the city government. Each time, it successfully reminded the Anchorage community that the local government also serves Out North's artists and audience and not just those who protest Out North's programs.

In the summer of 1997, Out North learned that the Anchorage Assembly was considering rejecting a recommendation to fund Out North's ONSTAGE project, a theater program designed as a delinquency prevention service for at-risk youth.

From the beginning, Out North tracked the votes for and against its funding. As the time for assembly action came closer, it was clear Out North did not have the votes to keep its funding. Out North concentrated its efforts on the public presentation it was entitled to make to the assembly. It asked a broad cross-section of its supporters to speak—twelve speakers including conservative friends of assembly members, parents, business people, and the staff who ran the project—insuring that each speaker would offer a different viewpoint. It aimed to proudly show the assembly who Out North is: people of color, people with disabilities, people who are lesbian or gay, people of all ages, Christians and atheists.

Out North's presentation proved effective. Two of the conservative members of the assembly voted with a 6-5 majority in its favor.

Out North then said thank you—with letters to the editor, personal letters to both sides of the assembly, and personal calls to the assembly members who saved its funding. It informed its supporters and the public about what happened and worked toward ensuring that the assembly member who switched his vote continued getting positive constituent response.

Out North, continues its struggle to receive local governmental support. However, having a ready group of supporters willing to speak for them at public hearings insures that at least its voice is being heard.

Media Advocacy

Using the media to mobilize public support is a strategic decision that should be made after careful consideration with the individuals and groups involved in the challenge. Dealing with the media is time-consuming, and you cannot control what a journalist will report. Media attention potentially can inflate an incident into something much more public and contentious than you ever intended.

But even if you decide not to actively engage the media, you should prepare for the likelihood that they will contact you.

Develope a Media Strategy

Before speaking to the media, you and allied groups should develop a unified media strategy. Most importantly, you need to determine how to frame the issues and what you hope to achieve in telling your story.

This handbook provides general guidelines. The course you choose will depend on the particular nature and circumstances of the challenge. Organizations such as NCFE can assist you with media advocacy and help you develop your media strategy. There are also progressive public relations groups that assist public interest and nonprofit organizations by providing media training and media consulting services. See Appendix II for more information about these organizations.

Develop Your Message

Develop a strong key message. Condense your issue into three strategic points: the problem, the solution, and the call to action. Take charge of the debate so that it is conducted on your terms, with your words, and with your metaphors. Select and organize the key pieces of information to tell the story you want to tell. Be sure that all your allies communicate the same basic message.

Broaden the debate beyond discussion of the work under attack. Question the attempt to "impose a moral agenda" or "stifle dialogue." Champion the "rights of artists and audience members in a free society." Be very clear about why the public should care about these issues. Emphasize the value of the artist or the organization to the community. Appear more reasonable than your opponents but don't belittle their concerns.

Stick to your message. Don't answer reporters' questions, respond to them with your key points. Use your key points to maintain control and direct the interview. As distasteful as the notion of "sound bites" may be, short and concise sentences help insure the reporter gets your quotation down exactly as you said it. Avoid being overly subtle and forcing a reporter to read between the lines of your comments. Be very careful when using sarcasm; it reads poorly. Don't be afraid to say "I don't know" or "I'll get back to you" or to refer a reporter to someone who is better able to respond to a question.

Identify and Contact Members of the Media

Most communities have several media outlets, including daily and weekly newspapers and television and radio stations. Target the reporters. Identify which reporters—arts, legal, local, or other—would be most interested in the story. Respect deadlines and be timely, friendly, and sensitive. Pitch your story as compelling, controversial, and new. Follow up with any journalists who cover the incident. Keep them updated as the situation develops. Maintain a press file for all the coverage you do receive.

Create a Media Release

Media releases and press statements provide reporters with the essential details of the challenge and succinctly communicate your message. An entire release or statement should be no more than two pages and should include a contact name and phone number. Start with a headline that states your position affirmatively. State what you support and what you are doing, not only what you oppose. Follow with a strong lead that states your key message; avoid presenting information chronologically and burying important issues or facts in the middle of the statement. Follow your key message with essential background information. Include statements by allies and community leaders that can be lifted by reporters as quotations. Include a brief description of your organization or your credentials as an artist. The release must establish the credibility of the artist or organization.

Peg your media release to coincide with an important event such as a vote or demonstration. Plan ahead. Media releases can take up to 10 days to be processed. Even releases by fax should be sent three to four days ahead of time.

An example of a media release is included in Appendix III.

Respond to Media Coverage

Letters to the editor can be an effective way to respond to articles and editorials about a challenge to freedom of artistic expression. Letters should be brief. Most editors will print only a portion of your letter, so include only essential information. Also include your name, telephone number, and address so that the editor can verify that you wrote the letter. Most newspapers will not print unverified letters. Refer to the article or editorial to which you are responding. A letter to the editor thanking the newspaper for positive coverage is an effective way to amplify the effect of that coverage.

You may want to submit an op-ed piece to your newspaper, articulating your position in your own words. Or consider soliciting an op-ed from a person outside your organization who can frame the issues in a larger context. Contact the editorial staff to learn the submission procedures and guidelines.

Consider Legal Options

Responding to a challenge to freedom of artistic expression by filing a lawsuit is risky. Litigation is exhausting, frustrating, contentious, expensive, and slow. Cases can take several years to resolve. The general public tends to respond poorly to litigation. Also, you are limited in what relief the court can grant you should it rule in your favor. Monetary damages are difficult to prove. Of course there are no guarantees—no matter how strong your case—that you will win.

But litigation can be extremely rewarding and may be the only way to halt a long-standing practice of censorship or a legislative enactment. You may vindicate not only your own rights, but the rights of your entire community and perhaps even the rights of artists nationally. Sometimes government officials will respond only if there is a real threat of litigation. And if you need immediate action, one of the law's emergency procedures such as a temporary restraining order may be available to you.

It is essential to consult with an attorney familiar with First Amendment law if you are considering litigation. Not every challenge will give rise to a legally cognizable claim. Most litigation will arise from challenges by, or decisions of, public officials. These challenges are the ones that most directly implicate the First Amendment.

You also may be able to sue if the terms of your exhibition, performance, or rental contract were not followed. But read your contracts carefully. Some contracts will allow presenters or site managers to cancel an event for stated reasons. These conditions may be enforceable. The contracts may also specify that disputes be resolved through arbitration, rather than in court.

Attacks by private persons and entities are rarely addressable by litigation. Indeed, private individuals have the First Amendment right to voice their distaste for your artistic expression. Respond to these attacks with the grassroots and media advocacy tools described above.

Resolutions

What does it mean to successfully resolve a challenge to freedom of expression? It might mean that the exhibition or performance goes on as planned. However, it might also mean that some mutually agreeable compromise is reached, or compensation is paid. Or it might mean that meaningful and educational dialogue took place or that long-term relationships and understanding were established. Even if you decide to litigate, you will often need to devise a resolution to address any residual effects of the court's decision.

Be creative in working out resolutions. Consider alternative presentation venues, especially if you can get assurances that visitors to the original display space will be directed to the relocated work. Consider suggesting a public discussion or the distribution of explanatory materials that address your opposition's concerns. Work for arrangements that will support long-term solutions within your community, instead of those that address only the particular challenge. Indeed, sometimes these can be more favorable outcomes than merely keeping an exhibit open.

FIGURE 18

Caterine Clay's Notice of Protest

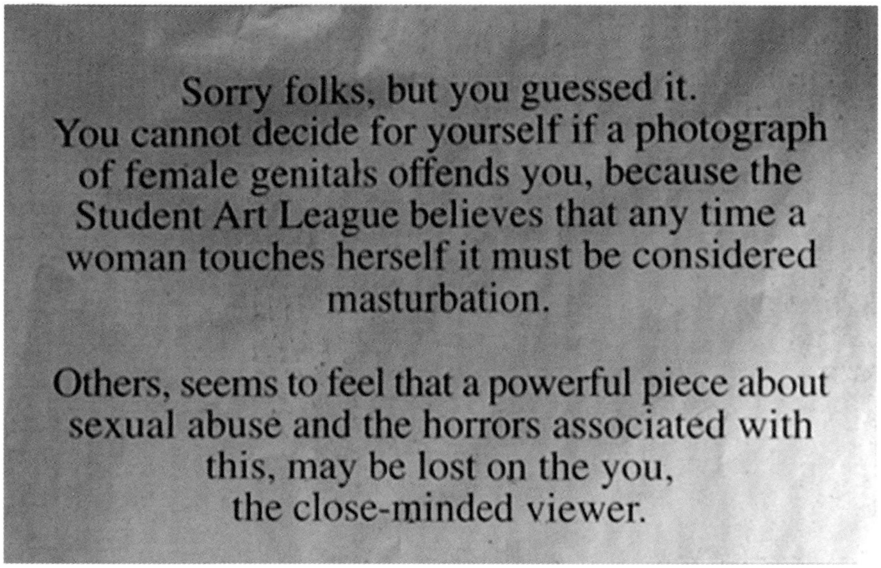

Replace Art with Notice of Protest

A commentary on female genital mutilation, showing the artist's hand touching her nude crotch, was removed from a student exhibition at the University of Louisville in Kentucky. Officers of the student art league that oversaw the exhibit declared the work and two others by Catherine Clay to be "offensive and insensitive." Clay replaced the image with a statement of protest (Fig. 18).

Explain the Art to the Audience

A banner created by five Filipino-American artists known as Grupo de Gago was reinstalled in a public building in Los Angeles after the organizers of the festival for which the banner was produced agreed to be present at the exhibit at all times to "insure informed dialogue" among the artists, the festival committee, and the public. The banner depicted a dog being roasted on a spit, a swastika, a star of David, a rosary, and a monkey. The Los Angeles Cultural Affairs Department had ordered the removal of the banner because they thought it was "necessary to show cultural sensitivity when a banner is to be hung in a public building."

Hold a Public Forum

The Ohio University Lancaster Branch Campus held a public forum to discuss the views raised by critics of the exhibit Valentine's Day '93 at the university's Visual Arts Gallery. Over four hundred people and several media representatives attended the forum. The exhibit had been attacked by the Fairfield Family Association, which considered several entries in the exhibit to be "homoerotic porn masquerading as an art display."

Conclusion

Mary Ann Peters
President NCFE Board of Directors

Very few artists imagine themselves in a censorship debate. And rarely do they anticipate the insults and innuendos that give censorship its demeaning theatrics. To foster an atmosphere of creative thinking it is important to understand that artistic endeavor is reliant upon equal parts courage and talent. I am confident that this handbook will provide the necessary tools to override the backlash that corrodes our confidence in a censorial exchange. And perhaps more importantly, to intercept the argument before it begins. As an artist and President of the Board of NCFE, there is no doubt in my mind that this guide will be an immeasurable asset to free expression for years to come.

"Censorship reflects a society's lack of confidence in itself. It is a hallmark of an authoritarian regime. Long ago those who wrote our First Amendment charted a different course. They believed a society can be truly strong only when it is truly free. In the realm of expression they put their faith, for better or for worse, in the enlightened choice of the people, free from interference of a policeman's intrusive thumb or a judge's heavy hand. So it is that the Constitution protects coarse expression as well as refined, and vulgarity no less than elegance. A book worthless to me may convey some value to my neighbor. In the free society to which our Constitution has committed us, it is for each to choose for himself."

—Justice Potter Stewart,
Ginzburg v. United States, 383 U.S. 463
(1966) (dissenting)

What to Do If It Happens to You

A CHECKLIST

1. Get the Facts

- Identify precisely the work being challenged. One piece? An entire exhibit? Certain lyrics to a song? A title? A theme?
- Identify the challengers. Organized group? Member of the public? Public official? Arts council? Gallery board of directors? University administration?
- Identify the reason for the challenge. Sexuality? Nudity? Religion? Racial issues? Nationalism? Identity of the artist?
- Identify the location of the challenge. Public gallery or theater? Private exhibition hall? Park? Your own home?
- Identify when all key events occurred and when all key decisions were made. When was the complaint made? When was a decision to cancel or remove the work made? When were/are funding decisions finalized?
- Identify those involved in important decisions. Who decides/decided whether to remove the artwork? Can anyone override that decision?
- Identify avenues of appeal.
- Determine your desired resolution.

Create a fact sheet containing all this information.

2. Notify Involved Parties

Meet with staff and board to explain the situation.

3. *Inform & Enlist the Support of Key Allies*

Contact local and national arts, anti-censorship, and advocacy organizations.

4. *Mobilize Community Support*

- Identify allies within your community.
- Organize public discussion.
- Mount letter-writing campaigns.
- Hold public demonstrations.

5. *Confront the Challengers*

- Write letters defending your work and the principle of freedom of expression.
- Attend public hearings and decision-making sessions.

6. *Media Advocacy*

- Develop a media strategy.
  - ✓ Condense your issue into three points: the problem, the solution, and the call to action.
  - ✓ Create a media release: Provide the media with a brief summary of the important events and deliver your message.
  - ✓ Identify and contact members of the media.
  - ✓ Be prepared to deal with the public: both the general public and your audience and supporters.
  - ✓ Respond to media coverage.

7. *Consider Legal Options*

Consult with an attorney if you think your legal rights have been violated.

8. *Devise a Creative Solution*

Be creative in working out a resolution with which you are happy.

Organizations

Advocacy

National Campaign for Freedom of Expression

(202) 393-2787 or (800) 477-6233
918 F Street, NW
Suite 609
Washington, D.C. 20004
www.ncfe.net

NCFE maintains a hotline for artists and arts organizations to report challenges to freedom of artistic expression. NCFE provides advocacy support, including media advocacy, with respect to specfic challenges and helps artists and arts communities organize to promote artistic freedom. NCFE also acts a liaison between the arts community and the national civil liberties community. The NCFE Quarterly reports on challenges and examines current issues of free speech and artistic freedom.

National Coalition Against Censorship

(212) 807-6222
275 Seventh Ave.
New York, N.Y. 10001
www.ncac.org

NCAC is a broad-based coalition of national, nonprofit organizations, including religious, educational, artistic, labor, professional, and civil rights groups, dedicated to fighting censorship. Founded in 1974, NCAC engages in public education and advocacy at national, state, and local levels. NCAC monitors controversies; acts as a clearinghouse; organizes meetings and conferences; provides analyses, strategies, research, referrals, and speakers; publishes newsletters and policy papers; and provides information to lawyers, scholars, journalists, and the general public. The organization provides direct assistance to individuals and groups fighting censorship battles. NCAC encourages grassroots activism in support of the First Amendment and has a large network of activists, including a working group on women, censorship and "pornography," which opposes censorship from a feminist perspective.

(800) 743-6768
2000 M Street, NW
Suite 400
Washington, D.C. 20036
www.pfaw.org

People for the American Way/artsave Project

Founded in 1980 by Norman Lear and a group of civic and religious leaders, People for the American Way was established to help strengthen our national commitment to the spirit of community. As part of its mission, People For strives to advance fundamental rights, including freedom of expression, freedom of religion, and respect for cultural pluralism. The organization combines research, education, and technical and legal assistance to promote freedom of expression and combat censorship in a variety of media. It publishes Artistic Freedom Under Attack, a comprehensive survey of arts censorship incidents, vols. 1-4, and its artsave project monitors, publicizes, and counters attacks on artistic expression through legal and technical assistance to artists and arts institutions. PFAW also publishes Protecting the Freedom to Learn which provides legal and technical assistance to educators and parents facing censorship challenges in their communities and local schools.

One of the following organizations may be helpful depending on the particular artwork being challenged and your specific situation:

(503) 797-6988
2325 East Burnside Street
Portland, OR 97214
www.artistcommunities.org

Alliance of Artists Communities

The Alliance of Artistic Communities is a national service organization that supports the field of artists communities and residency programs. It does this by encouraging collaboration among members of the field, providing leadership on field issues, setting professional standards, raising the visibility of artists communities and promotes philanthropy in the field.

(404) 577-1079
1083 Austin Ave., NE
Atlanta, GA 30307
home.earthlink.net/~altroots1

Alternate ROOTS

Alternate ROOTS, a membership service organization based in the Southeast, supports the creation and presentation of original performing art that is rooted in a particular community of place, tradition, or spirit. ROOTS is committed to social and economic justice and the protection of the natural world, and addresses those concerns through its services and programs.

(202) 737-5900
1012 14th Street NW, Suite 500,
Washington, D.C. 20005
www.igc.apc.org/aaup

American Association of University Professors

The association's mission is the protection and advancement of academic freedom in American colleges and universities and the promotion of teaching and research.

American Booksellers Foundation for Free Expression

The American Booksellers Foundation for Free Expression, formed in 1990, aims to inform and educate booksellers, other members of the book industry, and the public about the deleterious effects of censorship; and to actively promote and protect the free expression of ideas, particularly freedom in the choice of reading material.

(914) 591-BOOK x.267
828 South Broadway
Tarrytown, N.Y. 10591
www.bookweb.org/abffe

American Library Association Office for Intellectual Freedom

The Office for Intellectual Freedom is charged with implementing the intellectual freedom policies of the American Library Association. The specific goal of the office is to educate librarians and the public about the importance of the concept, as embodied in the Bill of Rights. The office publishes the bimonthly Newsletter on Intellectual Freedom, the Intellectual Freedom Manual, and Censorship and Selection: Issues and Answers for Schools.

(312) 280-4223
50 East Huron
Chicago, IL 60611
www.ala.org

Artisits for a Hate Free America

AHFA is a nonprofit organization working through the music industry to counter the effects of bigotry, censorship, racism, and homophobia in American politics and public life. AHFA educates and mobolizes young people to work, love, and vote hate-free.

800-3what-2do
244 Madison Ave., Suite 353
New York, NY 10016

Asian American Arts Alliance

Asian American Arts Alliance is a not-for-profit arts service organization founded in 1983 to increase the support, recognition, and appreciation of Asian American arts. The Arts Alliance strives to assist Asian American artists and their groups, and raise awareness of the diversity of Asian American arts and cultures. They provide information services, networking and advocacy services, and professional assistance through publications, technical assistance, public forums and roundtables, referrals, and a resource library. Publications include Resource Directory, a bi-monthly Asian American Arts Calendar/Resources & Opportunities, and Dialogue, a bilingual Asian American arts magazine.

(212) 941-9208
74 Varick Street
Suite 302
New York, N.Y. 10013
www.aaartsalliance.org

Association of American Publishers

AAP is the national trade association of the U.S. book publishing industry. Among AAP's primary concerns are the protection of intellectual property rights in all media and the defense of free expression and freedom to publish at home and abroad.

(202) 232-3335
1718 Connecticut Ave., NW, 7th Flr
Washington, D.C. 20009
www.publishers.org

Association of American University Presses

(212) 941-6610
584 Broadway, Suite 410
New York, NY 10012
aaup.uchicago.edu/aaup_home.html

AAUP is a cooperative, nonprofit organization of university presses. Formally established in 1937, the organization promotes the work and influence of university presses, provides cooperative marketing efforts, and helps its presses respond to the changing economy and environment.

Association of Independent Video and Filmmakers

(212) 807-1400
304 Hudson Street
Sixth Floor
New York, NY 10013
www.aivf.org

AIVF aims to increase the creative and professional opportunities for independent video and filmmakers, to ensure and enhance the growth of independent media by providing services, advocacy and information, and promoting diversity and democracy in the communication and expression of ideas and images.

Association of Performing Arts Presenters

(202) 833-2787
1112 16th Street NW, Suite 400
Washington, D.C. 20036
www.artspresenters.org

The Association of Performing Arts Presenters is an international service organization with over 1,600 members in the United States and Canada ranging from large performing arts centers in major urban areas to small presenting groups in rural communities.

Atlatl, Inc.

(602) 277-3711
P.O. Box 34090
Phoenix, AZ 85067
atlatl@artswire.org

Atlatl, a national service organization for Native American artists, exists to promote the vitality of contemporary Native American arts.

College Art Association

(212) 691-1051
275 Seventh Avenue
New York, NY 10001
www.collegeart.org

The College Art Association, founded in 1911, promotes the highest standards of scholarship and teaching in the history and criticism of the visual arts and the highest levels of creativity and technical skill in the teaching and the practices of art.

Council of Literary Magazines and Presses

(212) 741-9110
154 Christopher Street, Suite 3C
New York, NY 10014

CLMP is a national organization whose mission is to preserve, promote, and support independent noncommercial literary magazines and presses through services and programs for members including technical assistance, research and development, advocacy, information services, and other initiatives.

Dance Theater Workshop

Dance Theater Workshop is a not-for-profit, community-based organization that provides artist sponsorship programs and production facilities as well as a broad spectrum of administrative, promotional, and technical services to the community of independent artists.

(212) 691-6500
219 W. 19th Street
New York, NY 10011
www.dtw.org

Dance/USA

Dance/USA is a national service organization that speaks for dance and acts as a forum to advance the art of dance.

(202) 833-1717
1156 15th Street NW, Suite 820
Washington, D.C. 20005-1704
www.danceusa.org

Feminists for Free Expression

Feminists for Free Expression is a group of diverse feminists working to preserve the individual's right and responsibility to read, hear, view, and produce materials of her choice, without the intervention of the state "for her own good."

(212) 702-6292
2525 Times Square Station
New York, N.Y. 10108
www.well.com/user/freedom

Freedom to Read Foundation

The Freedom to Read Foundation promotes and defends First Amendment rights to express ideas without government interference, and to read and listen to the ideas of others, particularly through library collections. The foundation challenges the constitutionality of laws that inhibit the exercise of those rights. Through participation as a party or an amicus in important First Amendment litigation, the foundation supports the rights of libraries and librarians to include in their collections and to disseminate to the public any work that has not previously been declared illegal.

(312) 280-4226
50 East Huron, Chicago, IL 60611
www.ala.org/alaorg/oif/ftrf

International Sculpture Center

The International Sculpture Center is a nonprofit service organization for sculptors and others significantly involved in sculpture. Established in 1960, the ISC works to create a stable environment for sculptors by providing them with opportunities and by encouraging the development and advancement of three-dimensional art. Services include biennial international conferences and technical workshops, publications, computerized sculpture registry, and exhibition services.

(202) 785-1144
1050 17th Street NW, Suite 250
Washington, D.C. 20036
www.sculpture.org

The Literary Network

(212) 741-9110
154 Christopher Street, Suite 3C
New York, NY 10014
www.gmu.edu/departments/awp/litnet.html

The Literary Network, cosponsored by 15 nonprofit literary presses and organizations, is designed to inform and mobilize the field of literature on issues pertaining to the freedom of expression, with special focus on the controversy surrounding the National Endowment for the Arts.

Massachusetts Music Industry Coalition

(978) 537-1669
www.ultranet.com/~crowleyn/what.html

Mass. M.I.C. is a nonprofit organization dedicated to promoting and protecting the freedom of musical expression in Massachusetts and nationwide. The organization is a coalition of musicians, fans, promoters, music media, and music industry professionals.

Media Coalition

(212) 587-4025
139 Fulton Street, Suite 302
New York, N.Y. 10038

The Media Coalition, founded in 1973, is an association that defends the right to produce, distribute, and sell First Amendment protected materials.

National Association of Artists' Organizations

(202) 347-6350
918 F Street NW, Suite 611
Washington, D.C. 20004

NAAO is a nonprofit membership organization dedicated to serving and promoting artist-run organizations: the primary supporters, presenters, and makers of new and emerging work in the visual, performing, media, literary, and interdisciplinary arts. NAAO provides a national voice advocating for cultural equity, freedom of expression, individual artists, and the organizations that serve them.

National Association of Latino Arts and Culture

(210) 227-1432
1300 Guadeloupe Street
San Antonio, TX 78207
nalacarts@aol.com

NALAC is an emerging arts service organization formed to serve the unique needs of the diverse Latino arts and cultural communities throughout the United States. The primary focus of the organization is to provide leadership in advocacy of national policy issues that impact the Latino arts and cultural communities across the nation.

National Alliance for Media Arts and Culture

NAMAC is an association of organizations and individuals dedicated to building a broad, common vision of diversity and equity, decentralization, and participation in the media arts—audio, video, film, and new multimedia technologies. NAMAC's aims include making media arts organizations an integral part of the community; ensuring that independent media artists from all cultural communities receive the recognition and support they merit; integrating media into all levels of education and promoting media literacy as an educational goal; promoting humane uses of and individual access to current and future media technologies; and encouraging media arts that are rooted in communities as well as those that are global in outlook.

(415) 431-1391
346 9th Street
San Francisco, CA 94103
www.namac.org

National Assembly of State Arts Agencies

NASAA is a membership organization representing the 56 arts agencies of the 50 states and six special jurisdictions of the United States.

(202) 347-6352
1029 Vermont Ave NW, Second Flr
Washington, D.C. 20005
www.nasaa-arts.org

National Gay and Lesbian Task Force

NGLTF is a civil rights organization building a movement to promote freedom and full equality for all lesbians and gay men.

(202) 332-6483
2320 17th Street, NW
Washington, D.C. 20009-2702
www.ngltf.org

National Performance Network

The National Performance Network is a program conceived as a means to support the work and creative processes of a national community of artists in dance, theater, music, performance art and puppetry in all regions of the United States. The network is a consortium of 58 cultural organizations.

(212) 645-6200
54 W 21st Street, Suite 501
New York, NY 10010

National Writers Union, UAW Local 1981, AFL-CIO

The NWU promotes and protects the rights, interests, and economic advancement of members; organizes writers to improve professional working conditions through collective bargaining actions; and provides professional services to members.

(212) 254-0279
113 University Place, Sixth Floor
New York, NY 10003
www.nwu.org/nwu

PEN American Center

(212) 334-1660
568 Broadway, 4th Floor
New York, NY 10012
www.pen.org

PEN American Center is the largest of 130 centers that make up International PEN. Founded in London in 1921 by John Galsworthy to foster understanding among men and women of letters in all countries, International PEN is the only worldwide organization of writers and the chief voice of the literary community. Members of PEN work for freedom of expression wherever it has been endangered; the PEN Freedom-to-Write Committee issues a bimonthly bulletin.

Society for Photographic Education

(303) 492-0588

The Society for Photographic Education is a nonprofit, membership organization that provides a forum for the discussion of photography as a means of creative cultural expression and cultural insight.

Theatre Communications Group

(212) 697-5230
355 Lexington Ave.
New York, NY 10017
www.tcg.org

Theatre Communications Group is the national organization for nonprofit professional theatre.

Legal Support

American Civil Liberties Union

The ACLU is a nonprofit, nonpartisan public interest organization devoted exclusively to protecting the basic civil liberties of all Americans, and extending them to groups that have traditionally been denied those rights. The mission of the ACLU is to assure that guarantees against unwanted governmental control in the Bill of Rights are respected and preserved for each new generation. In the area of the First Amendment, the ACLU works to preserve religious liberty, separation of church and state, and freedom of expression, association, and assembly.

(Contact your local affiliate—see www.aclu.org)

Center for Constitutional Rights

Center for Constitutional Rights was founded in 1966 by attorneys dedicated to the creative use of law as a positive force for social change. Among CCR's programs is the Movement Support Network, an anti-repression project that monitors surveillance of progressive organizations and activists by government and private agencies; provides advice and legal assistance to groups and individuals targeted by government agencies; and alerts Congress and the media to instances and trends in repression.

(212) 614-6464
666 Broadway
New York, N.Y. 10012

Gay & Lesbian Alliance Against Defamation

The Gay and Lesbian Alliance Against Defamation is a national organization that promotes fair, accurate, and inclusive representation of individuals and events in all media as a means of combating homophobia and all forms of discrimination based on sexual orientation or identity.

(212) 807-1700
150 West 26th Street, Suite 503
New York, N.Y. 10001

LAMBDA Legal Defense and Education Fund

LAMBDA, founded in 1973, works to defend and extend the rights of lesbians and gay men through test case litigation and public education.

(212) 809-8585
120 Wall Street, Suite 1500
New York, N.Y. 10005

Thomas Jefferson Center for the Protection of Free Expression

The Thomas Jefferson Center for the Protection of Free Expression devoted to the defense of free expression in all its forms: it is as concerned with the musician as with the mass media, with the painter as with the publisher and with the sculptor as with the editor. The Thomas Jefferson Center has close ties with the University of Virginia, but is an autonomous, not-for-profit entity.

(804) 295-4784
400 Peter Jefferson Place
Charlottesville, VA 22911-8691
www.tjcenter.org

(212) 319-2787
1 E. 53rd St.
6th Floor
New York, NY 10022

Volunteer Lawyers for the Arts

Volunteer Lawyers for the Arts has a national network of over forty independent VLAs throughout the United States and Canada providing legal services and assistance to artists and arts organizations in all creative fields who cannot afford private counsel.

Public Relations

(202)638-1431
529 14th Street, NW
Washington, DC 20045

American Forum

The American Forum helps organizations place op-eds and other media articles in news outlets around the country.

(303)292-1524
1836 Blake Street, Suite 100B
Denver, CO 80202

Cause Communications

Provides media training workshops to non-profit organizations and citizens interested in public interest issues.

(202) 326-8700
1333 H Street, NW #700
Washington, D.C. 20005

Communications Consortium Media Center

CCMC is a public interest media center dedicated to helping nonprofit organizations use media and telecommunications technologies as tools for public education and policy change. CCMC's work is focused on a cluster of issues: children and families, health care, gender equality, reproductive rights, global population, the environment, voting rights, civil rights, and immigration. Projects typically last one to five years and are individually supported financially.

(608) 257-4626
409 East Main Street
Madison, WI 53703

The Progressive Media Project

Helps individuals and groups publish op-eds in newspapers around the country.

225 West 57th Street
Suite 801
New York, NY 10019

ProMedia

Provides public interest media consulting for larger and smaller non-profit groups.

Riptide Communications, Inc.
Provides public interest media consulting.

(212)260-5000
666 Broadway, Suite 444
New York, NY 10012

SPIN (Institute for Alternative Journalism)
The SPIN Project at the Institute for Alternative Journalism offers free media advocacy consulting and training for progressive, nonprofit organizations.

(415) 284-1412
77 Federal St.
San Francisco, CA 94107
www.mediademocracy.org

Internet Resources

ArtsWire	www.artswire.org
FearNoArt dot com	www.fearnoart.com
Free Expression Clearinghouse	www.freeexpression.org
Rock Out Censorship	www.theroc.org
Fileroom	www.aaup.uic.edu/fileroom/documents/homepage.html

Making the News: A guide for Nonprofits & Activists
by Jason Salzman (Westview Press, 1998) is a very useful reference for media advocacy. Its resource section provides references to other media how-to books, sources for lists of news outlets, news media watchdog groups, media literacy organizations, communications consultants, and information on community organizing and fundraising.

Sample Documents

PART I
Sample Statements of Artistic Freedom Principles

Iowa Arts Council Statement on Freedom of Expression

The mission of the Iowa Arts Council is to promote the value, practice and appreciation of the arts and to develop a climate in which they flourish. Support of free speech is the centerpiece of this mission. The council is an advocate for and defender of the right of free speech by all citizens under the First Amendment of the Constitution of the United States.

The Iowa Arts Council recognizes the need for public support of the arts and understands the responsibilities that accompany the allocation of public funds. The council seeks the advice of qualified Iowans through the use of review panels for funding recommendations. The council is committed to uphold and maintain the highest artistic standards and to encourage excellence in the arts.

The council respects the integrity of an artist's personal vision and right to freedom of expression. The council rejects all attempts to control or censor the arts. Recognizing the diversity of viewpoints represented by Iowa communities, the council supports freedom of choice and access to the arts by all citizens.

Seattle Women's Caucus for Art Policy Concerning Censorship of Exhibitions

In keeping with the policies recommended by the National WCA exhibition committee, the Seattle chapter of the Women's Caucus for Art has established the following guidelines concerning censorship of members' artwork in any exhibitions sponsored or promoted by this chapter.

National WCA policy:

"All exhibitions associated with WCA should actively oppose censorship in any form. No exhibition associated with WCA should by action, statement or omission censor or appear to censor art created by women for consideration and inclusion in the exhibit."

SWCA GUIDELINES:

1. We will not remove artwork from WCA exhibitions based upon complaints from the public or staff of the exhibition space because of content. The removal of said artwork constitutes censorship.

2. We will not include non–WCA members on the exhibition committee for the purpose of curating exhibitions unless they are invited guest curators with a knowledge of art and art history.

3. Members of the WCA may present to the public and space staff a presentation of artwork with explanation and dialogue. Such dialogue assumes that much of people's overreaction to the artwork comes from fear and lack of familiarity with the content of women's art. The intent of this process is to empower, to enable viewers to think critically and positively about the relationship of art to their own lives.

Philosophy of the SWCA concerning exhibiting members' art:

Women artists' representations of themselves challenges the absolute authority of the tradition, often creating subversions which can support women's efforts at liberation. If the point of feminism is to find the politics of our personal lives, we need to create and develop spaces for feminist artists to visualize our lives. Censorship does not support the purpose of the WCA.

New School for Social Research Statement on Freedom of Artistic Expression

The University's policy on the free exchange of ideas states that, "an abiding commitment to preserving and enhancing freedom of speech, thought, inquiry and artistic expression is deeply rooted in the history of the New School for Social Research." The University's responsibility for and dedication to securing the conditions in which freedom of artistic expression can flourish extend to all forms of artistic expression, including fine arts, design, literature, and the performance of drama, music, and dance.

The opportunity to display or perform works of art at the University is made available through several academic processes and procedures in which faculty members and other duly appointed individuals exercise their best professional judgment. Among these procedures are selection of student artwork by faculty, selection of works by the Committee on the University Art Collection, display or performance as part of an approved curriculum. Such authorized display or performance, regardless of how unpopular the work might be, must be unhindered and free from coercion. Members of the University community and guests must reflect in their actions a respect for the right to communicate ideas artistically and must refrain from any act that would cause that right to be abridged. At the same time, the University recognizes that the right of artists to exhibit or perform does not preclude the right of others to take exception to particular works of art. However, this later right must be exercised in ways that do not prevent a work of art from being seen and must not involve any form of intimidation, defacement, or physical violence. The University rejects the claim of any outside individual or agency to dictate on the appropriateness or acceptability of the display or performance of any work of art in its facilities or a part of its educational programs.

PART II
Fact Sheet

In 1996, the Federal Way (WA) School District , near Seattle, banned the GAP Theatre Company following a presentation of "The View From Here" at the Federal Way High School. The production dealt with issues relating to gender equity, sexual harassment, and sexual orientation discrimination. The ban came after the Christian Coalition of Washington and a local talk radio host claimed the production was hostile to families and "traditional values." The superintendent justified the ban by asserting that the school district "should not be in the business of promoting alternative lifestyles."

Chronology of Events for the Federal Way Controversy

March 4, 1996	Preview show with discussion with Federal Way Health Advisory Committee
April 29, 1996	Community Performance at Truman High School for Federal Way Community members
April 30, 1996	G.A.P. confirms by telephone with Janine Green at Federal Way High School two shows at Federal High School. Carrie Gibson (CG) specifically talks about discussion period that will follow show.
May 10, 1996	G.A.P. performs the play *The View From Here* at Mercer Island High School. A student talks about her religious beliefs during discussion and Rick Turner, actor, responds respectfully about the effect of people's judgments on his willingness to share his life with those people.
May 16, 1996	Mercer Island High School Student is on KVI for two hours saying she was verbally attacked by a G.A.P. actor during discussion and was offended by a scene she described that did not occur in the play. KVI publicizes Federal Way shows on the air for several days following this broadcast.
May 28, 1996	G.A.P. performs *The View From Here* for two groups of sophomores and teachers in the health classes. The 2nd performance is attended by 8-10 people who told us they had heard of the show on KVI and did not have children in the district. At least one of them did not live in the district. Dave Welch, head of the Christian Coalition, also attended the show.

May 28, 1996	School Board meeting in the evening. Two school board members, Joel Marks and Ann Murphy, spoke out against G.A.P. presentation.
May 29, 1996	G.A.P. performs *The View From Here* at Truman High School in Federal Way.
May 29, 1996	CG received a call from Federal Way News reporter Sue Kidd. She wanted my reaction to School Board objections. She informed me of brewing controversy.
May 30, 1996	Several newspaper reporters called G.A.P. looking for our reaction to school district's decision to ban G.A.P.
May 31, 1996	CG calls Federal Way contact person to verify rumors about Federal Way's decision to ban us alleging that G.A.P. did not inform district about the discussion that follows show. Val Fimister confirms the district decision and agrees to fax memo from Asst Sup Tom Murphy to all principals.
June 3, 1996	CG receives fax copy of memo informing principals not to have G.A.P. back to school district.
June 3, 1996	CG calls Karen Stevens, district spokesperson, to get information and to propose another showing to the district management team for them to see the process in action. Call is not returned.
June 4, 1996	Tom Murphy, Asst Sup, returns CG's call and says that he will ask management team if there is any interest to see G.A.P. show. CG informs Tom Murphy about the content and process of the show as it has always been done.
June 10, 1996	School Board Meeting in Federal Way. Several citizens express concern over district's decision to "ban" G.A.P. Carolyn Hayek, AAUW member, offers her church as a place to see show and discussion.
June 11, 1996	Tom Murphy's assistant Nancy leaves voice mail saying, "district will not encourage or support" a performance of *The View From Here* in Federal Way.
June 12, 1996	CG confirms date for community performance with Carolyn Hayek at the Unitarian Universalist Church in Federal Way.

June 12, 1996	CG calls Tom Murphy to inform him of the scheduled date. Letter is sent by G.A.P. to Superintendent Tom Vander Ark explaining G.A.P.'s work, clarifying the misinformation and inviting him and other members of Federal Way to show.
June 25, 1996	G.A.P. performs The View From Here at Unitarian Universalist Church in Federal Way. 150 people attend. Discussion focuses on issues in play. At the end of the discussion G.A.P. actors answered questions about what occurred at high school performances. No one from the district attended the show.

Miami Arts Project

January 29, 1998

(Name and address omitted)

Dear (name omitted),

As per our conversation on Monday, below please find a recapitulation of the events surrounding the Nicole Eisenman controversy.

As you know, the Miami Arts Project was a two-city collaborative urban arts initiative. The participating institutions in Miami were: ArtCenter-South Florida, Dade County Aviation, Department of Fine Arts and Cultural Affairs, the Dade County Public School System and The Wolfsonian-FIU. In New York; The Drawing Center, Thread Waxing Space and StoreFront for Art and Architecture.

The projects were sited mainly in media spaces; we had 17 imaged on seventy-one billboards scattered throughout Dade County, Florida: nine public service announcements running on Channel 34, Miami Dade County Television done by New York artist Jocelyn Taylor, and an eight minute video by Miami artist Dara Friedman. The videos (including the public service announcements) are running at the Miami International Airport, Concourse D, near gate 2 (American Airlines Terminal). The only project that did not take place in a "media" space was the collaborative project by The Drawing Center and The Wolfsonian-FIU in which Nicole Eisenman painted a large wall mural in The Wolfsonian's fifth floor gallery.

The idea of the collaboration was that The Wolfsonian would curate their own exhibition entitled "Public Works" which was an exhibition of New Deal Mural Studies from their extensive collection and that their exhibition (which was completely funded by their own monies) be paired with a large scale wall mural executed by Nicole Eisenman. Nicole was invited by the Drawing Center as part of the Miami Arts Project. Her aspect of the exhibition at the Wolfsonian was covered by monies raised by the Miami Arts Project (including artist fee, material costs, jiffy lift, travel, etc. with the exception of lodging. Nicole stayed at The Wolfsonian's guest house).

The Miami Arts Project was initiated in April of 1995 and the projects "opened" on January 10th, 1998. Nicole went down to Miami to begin the execution of her mural the first two weeks of December, 1997. Prior to Nicole's visit to Miami, The Drawing Center had forwarded materials for review to The Wolfsonian: a description of what the mural would contain based on the information they had to date based on Nicole's ideas; a sketch, slides of Nicole's work including the mural she had done at The Drawing Center; articles and reviews on Nicole including a very extensive New York Times article that appeared in 1997. The Wolfsonian never asked to see a complete sketch or drawing. The only stipulation the Miami Arts Project put on the artist was that the mural somehow relate to Miami as its theme since all the projects (billboards and videos) were to have Miami as both the subject and content of the works.

(Name omitted), Curator at The Wolfsonian was the staff person who was supervising and coordinating Nicole's project with The Drawing Center. She had been fully apprised of Nicole' work, having seen photographs and slides of murals in New York executed by the artist. Nicole went down to Miami the first two weeks in December to execute her mural. She had been working on the mural while the curatorial staff (names omitted) looked on curious as to its progression. Ann Philbin, Director of The Drawing Center had had several conversations with (name omitted) as to Nicole's work and with specific reference to the acknowledgment that this mural could push the sensibility of The Wolfsonian and asked if The Wolfsonian could handle it. (Name omitted) stated that she was indeed familiar with the "racy" character and edge of Nicole's work and stated that she was nervous. Ann Philbin asked whether anyone else needed to understand or know about Nicole's work at The Wolfsonian and (name omitted) said something to the effect of "we will see what happens." This is significant to point out because The Wolfsonian's position has been that there was a breakdown in communication suggesting that it was initiated by The Drawing Center who had not fully communicated to them the content of Nicole's prior work while, in fact, the breakdown was within the internal ranks of The Wolfsonian.

After two weeks, Nicole completed her mural. The mural was painted on a gallery wall 30 feet high by 16 feet wide. The mural depicted an underwater scene in which huge muscle-bound men equipped with scuba and filmmaking gear , with cameras, lights and microphones are focusing in on a diminutive group; a daisy chain of cavorting lesbian sea monkeys engaged in anal and oral sex. Beforehand, Nicole had told (names omitted), (Founder and Chairman of the Board who had dined with Nicole one evening) that the center focus would be an orgy. Upon completion and after viewing the final product (names omitted) and staff became extremely upset with respect to the center of the mural which in actuality, spatially reflected the smallest section of the mural. This situation appears to have gone on for some time (roughly one hour) in which Nicole was subjected to verbal abuse by The Wolfsonian's Director and Chief Curator who kept repeating that their institution's state funding (because they had that summer merged with Florida International University, a large state school) was at serious risk and alluded that their jobs were at risk as well. In addition, they repeatedly stated that the content was "inappropriate" for school age children as they had already developed an educational program for Kindergarten through 12th grade revolving around both Nicole's mural and their respective exhibition. (A Junior High School class had already visited The Wolfsonian to watch Nicole in action while the mural was in progress. The students were told by the artist that the center would involve sex in some way in front of The Wolfsonian's Educational Coordinators). The situation between The Wolfsonian staff and the artist became heated. In light of what was occurring and in that specific context, Nicole agreed to change the mural. She re-painted the center (the objectionable part) in a witty response to what she was being asked to hide, with blue censor dots over what she thought were the objectionable parts of her mural by The Wolfsonian after a close review by (name omitted). After completion (name omitted) had left for California on a business trip), (name omitted) saw the mural and began saying that this was not acceptable since it would appear that The Wolfsonian was a censoring institution. She then went on to suggest, limb for limb, what Nicole should alter once again. Nicole did alter it and remove some of the sexual content of the mural, again, in a context that was not pleasant for her. Neither Ann Philbin from The Drawing

Center or myself as Project Director of the Miami Arts Project were informed as to the situation until after it had occurred and we were not reachable over that Saturday and Sunday.

Before this incident and in the process of painting the mural, (name omitted) had supplied the artist with a porn magazine of overweight women to use as a reference for the center part. In addition, (name omitted) had incited the artist on with respect to the "spicy" part of the mural having heard of the artist's reputation.

When Nicole arrived in New York shaken and disturbed, she had the opportunity to gather her thoughts with respect to this incident and the way she was treated (The Wolfsonian personally apologized for their comportment recognizing that it was, indeed, unacceptable behavior). I called (name omitted) to discuss the incident as did Ann Philbin. In separate conversations with both myself and Ann Philbin, (name omitted) admitted that they had acted inappropriately in respect to Nicole and that they had apologized. She went on to say that Nicole had made the changes "voluntarily" and that Nicole had the opportunity to walk away without making any changes. Nicole was actually being nice to The Wolfsonian, taking their fears to heart and feeling badly given the way they had framed the situation of losing state funding and allusions to job losses as well. There was no recognition of the context in which these changes were made and The Wolfsonian's role in these changes.

As a result of gathering her thoughts and reviewing the circumstances surrounding the changes, Nicole wrote a letter to (name omitted) (which you have a copy of) in which she stated her position, how the emotional situation and sense of coercion had affected her actions. All she asked in this letter was that The Wolfsonian acknowledge their role in the alteration of the mural by asking that a wall text, in the form of an Artist Note, be put up next to the mural stating:

"At the request of The Wolfsonian Institute, I have removed some of the sexual content of the mural entitled "Underwater Film Shoot". Nicole Eisenman.

This seemed to me to be a very reasonable request. She was acknowledging that she altered the mural at the request of this institution. The letter was dated December 22, 1997 and faxed and hard copied with carbon copies to myself, Ann Philbin, and Adine Varah, Esquire. On December 24, 1997 The Wolfsonian responded in the form of a letter from (name omitted) to Nicole (which you also have a copy) in which she maintains her position that Nicole offered to change the mural. In addition, she stated that the only object label that she would allow accompanying the mural was "After dialogue with The Wolfsonian, the artist agreed to alter the original concept for the mural." As you might imagine, this was unacceptable to Nicole since The Wolfsonian was not acknowledging their active role in the changes. Carbon copied on this letter were Paul Gallagher, Vice President, FIU, myself, Ann Philbin, Adine Varah, Esq. and Mitchell Wolfson, Jr. I received the letter on the 29th of December and called Nicole who was upset as to their suggested wall text proposal. I called (name omitted) on the 29th regarding this who informed me that I needed to take up this issue with (name omitted) directly which I did. We spoke for approximately one hour and a half in the afternoon, early evening. I listened to (name omitted) and what she had to say about the incident all over again. I tried to focus her in on the issue at hand which was not what had transpired but rather, the wall text and how it would read.

After an hour and a half of discussion it finally became clear to (name omitted) that I was not asking The Wolfsonian to write this wall text but rather, to have it printed as a quote from the artist which read:

"At the request of The Wolfsonian, I have removed some of the sexual content of the mural entitled "Underwater Film Shoot." Nicole Eisenman.

What she was previously arguing was that since, in her view, they had never "requested" the changes, saying that Nicole did them voluntarily, she (The Wolfsonian) would not put up that wall text. Finally, she understood that my request was an artist quote and not coming from her and she said that sounded fine to her but she needed to check with her two curators (names omitted) regarding this. I asked that she call me on Friday January 2, 1998. Friday came and went without any call. I called her that Monday January 5th, the day I was leaving to Miami for the Project. That Monday she agreed to put up the wall text saying after all, it was indeed, no big deal. On Tuesday morning from my sister's house in Miami, I confirmed this agreement by fax to her recognizing how this wall text had become a barrier for the artist, The Drawing Center and The Wolfsonian and not wishing any more conflict. (You have a copy of my fax). In it, I simply confirmed our oral agreement that The Wolfsonian would put up a wall label in the form of a quote from Nicole (the quote in the above paragraph).

Saturday came (January 10th), the day of the private opening for both Nicole's mural at The Wolfsonian and their respective exhibition. I went upstairs to the gallery where Nicole's mural was to check the wall text to make sure it was up and correct and it was not there. I pulled (name omitted) aside to ask her why it was not up and she simply said, "no, no" nodding her head and I looked at her and walked away in disbelief. I informed both Ann Philbin and Nicole (who had not yet entered The Wolfsonian and was waiting for me outside) that the wall text was not up. She became angry as did Ann Philbin, both in disbelief. I pulled (name omitted) outside to discuss the issue and we could not come to any agreement. (Name omitted) stated that she had never agreed with me to the wall text and that she merely said that she would try to accommodate it. When pressed as to why she had not contacted me that week in Miami with reference to her decision not to put it up, she stated that she did not know how to reach me in Miami (nor apparently did she make any effort to reach either Ann Philbin at The Drawing Center or the artist herself). Meanwhile, I had received numerous telephone calls from The Wolfsonian staff all that week at my sister's house to discuss the arrangements for our first panel discussion for the Miami Arts Project which was to take place at The Wolfsonian that day at 2:00 p.m.

The panel discussion, which was to discuss collaborative strategies for non-profit institutions moderated by Kevin Consey, Director of the Museum of Contemporary Art in Chicago became heated once the issue with reference to Nicole came out. The audience was actively engaged in the debate as were the panelists (which included (name omitted) and Ann Philbin). At the very end (name omitted) stood up to speak and mentioned that a wall text would indeed go up and that the wording would be worked out between The Wolfsonian and The Drawing Center.

The following week, Ann Philbin received a fax from (name omitted) showing an altered wall text by The Wolfsonian. The last two sentences read, "The mural presented here is a modified version of the artist's original concept. Some of its sexual content has been removed." Anne Philbin faxed back a letter on January 15, 1998 saying that, as they may have guessed, this was not acceptable to the artist but if they changed the last sentence to read, "Some of its sexual content has been removed at the request of The Wolfsonian", she (and the artist) would consider the issue resolved. However, she went on to state that if The Wolfsonian did not agree to this, Nicole would like to request that her mural be painted over in its entirety as soon as possible. In this event, The Drawing Center requested full documentation be made in advance of the work. At this point I was apprised of the situation (I was out of town until Thursday evening January 15th). I decided to ask our attorney, Steven Johnson, who is a board member of the Miami Arts Project, to get involved in an effort to come to an acceptable resolution for all. We had been apprised that this situation was now out of The Wolfsonian's hands and in the hands of FIU and their attorney. (The Wolfsonian had an emergency board meeting over this issue and I understand that the board came out in favor of (name omitted)'s actions and her handling of the situation. It is clear, however, that the Trustees were not accurately informed as to the details and agreements. Both sides were not factually represented). Steve spoke with their attorney. The attorney apprised Steve that FIU was having an emergency board meeting with reference to this issue on January 22nd. Steve was apprised on the 23rd that FIU backed the decision not to put up the wall text that (name omitted) had agreed to with me and that they keep the one which they now had in place. He did mention that they were open to suggestions as to the wording. When I was apprised of this, my feeling was that it was a waste of attorney time to "compromise" on language since there was a fundamental difference of views here and they would never recognize their role in these changes.

Nicole would like to request once again, that her mural be painted over and is in the process of drafting a letter to (name omitted) to that effect.

The press did not pick up on this. The first major article (which you have a copy of) came out in the Miami Herald on Wednesday, January 7th and another article, discussing the controversy, came out on Sunday, January 18th. I understand that several art magazines will be writing on this as well. I am faxing you the last article that came out in the Herald on January 18th (Ann Philbin was horrified when she read her quote in that article. It was taken out of context with reference to whether, in her opinion, The Wolfsonian had the right to ask for alterations to the mural. The reporter asked her a specific legal question which she then re-framed into a different context).

The issues which are extremely disturbing to me are as follows:

1. Censorship and its critical political, cultural and social implications.

2. Enormous breaches in professionalism.

    - That (name omitted) never communicated to her superiors information that was provided to her both visually and orally.

    - That she claims she never knew what the content of Nicole's mural was to be and that by making these claims she necessarily, implicitly portrayed The Drawing Center in an un-professional light.

- The fact that she has never publicly acknowledged that she knew and was involved with the development of the mural.

- The way in which Nicole was treated with tremendous disrespect.

- The way in which Ann Philbin and I were treated with disrespect and allusions of not having been professional, not having provided "disclosure" (as if there was anything to hide).

- That (name omitted) claimed she never agreed to put up the wall text.

- The fact that what was presented, in my opinion, to the Board of Trustees at The Wolfsonian and subsequently to the Board at Florida International University did not represent an accurate portrayal of the events and issues. The fact that FIU looked, in my opinion, only to the legal issues of liability and exposure and not to the ethical and moral issues associated with censorship and the looming issue of a complete breakdown in professionalism by their affiliated institution.

- And on a personal basis, I find it extremely disturbing that institutions in Miami seem to function under a veil of censorship (I could site you numerous examples just from my work as Project Director of the Miami Arts Project). The fact that censorship did not become a compelling issue for an educational institution such as FIU (which is state funded) to investigate is beyond my comprehension and speaks very poorly of our nation's educational system.

I believe I have provided you of a clear and accurate picture as to the events and issues. Please call me either at StoreFront (number omitted) or in the afternoons at home (number omitted) if you have any questions or need clarification and thank you once again (name omitted).

Kindly,
Cristina Delgado, Project Director

PART III
Coordinated Action Alert, Sign-On Letter & Media Release

Urgent Action Alert

SIGNATURES REQUESTED FOR LETTER STATING OPPOSITION TO CENSORSHIP OF MURAL IMAGES IN LOS ANGELES

As many of you are aware, the Social Art and Public Art Resource Center (SPARC), a nonprofit arts organization that coordinates public mural projects by urban youth, is embroiled in another censorship battle over one of its mural projects. This time the works raising the ire of local authorities are spray can art images that are part of an authorized and extensively planned mural in an area known as the Venice Graffiti Pit. The images at issue are a caricature of a pig in a blue uniform beating a spray can artist and a semi-nude female. The two murals were covered, first with tarps and then later with boards, after representatives from the LAPD and the community protested the images. SPARC artistic director Professor Judith F. Baca has been personally attacked, receiving death threats and an on-air condemnation by Rush Limbaugh.

A full summary of the incident is posted on www.freeexpression.org. The story was also covered in today's New York Times. Briefly, the murals were created after the Los Angeles Recreation and Parks Commission granted SPARC permission to paint the area. All of the images, including the two at the center of the current controversy, were preapproved by the Commission, and a Commission member was present as the images were being painted. The preapproval was only one stage in a complex planning process during which artists were recruited and the community surveyed about the mural.

In response to the complaints, the Commission, without informing SPARC, convened a hearing to discuss the controversy. SPARC attended the hearing anyway and called for mediation between the artists, police, interested community members and the Commission. SPARC indicated that the artists may be willing to modify their images. Nonetheless, the Commission decided to remove the images following the expiration of the 90-day notice period to which the artists are entitled under the federal Visual Artists Rights Act. That 90-day clock began ticking approximately September 2, 1997.

This is the third incident in the past year and a half in which the Commission and the Police Department have attempted to remove images from SPARC-coordinated murals.

We are urging the Commission to accept SPARC's offer of mediation. This is a very timely issue and we want to get the letter out as soon as possible. Please let me know ASAP if your organization would like to sign on or if you have any suggested modifications to the letter. If you can participate, please fax me a signature and let me know how you want to be identified. Also let me know if you'd like to sign on but need time to get approval. And lastly, CIRCULATE THIS SIGN-ON REQUEST TO ANY PERSON OR ORGANIZATION YOU THINK WOULD ENDORSE IT. Organizations dealing with Latino, youth and/or arts issues are especially relevant.

Recreation and Parks Commission

September 22, 1997

City Hall East
200 Main Street Room 1325
Los Angeles, CA 90012

Dear Commissioners:

The undersigned organizations, each dedicated to defending the fundamental right of freedom of expression, note our strong objection to your censorship of some of the images in the Venice Graffiti Pit and your refusal to talk to the artists about their images.

Regardless of whether the artists waived the rights granted to them by California Civil Code section 987, as you contend, the artists did not waive their First Amendment rights to free artistic expression. The First Amendment prohibits the government from placing viewpoint-based restrictions on expression. The Commission's censorship of these artistic images because it finds their viewpoint offensive violates the clear spirit of our nation's free speech heritage.

We understand that members of the community may have legitimate concerns about some of the images contained in the mural. However, we cannot understand why you continue to refuse to engage in a dialogue with the artists to discuss those concerns and explore a mutually acceptable resolution.

Your actions threaten to undo the monumental achievements of the Social Art & Public Art Resource Center (SPARC). SPARC was able to bring together a diverse group of the city's youth, many of them fierce rivals, to work on a common project. The mural provided these youth an outlet to express themselves — their feelings, beliefs, perceptions, frustrations, aspirations — in a constructive way. The project gave these young people the voice and a forum they are so frequently denied. SPARC and the artists were careful to comply with all the rules the Commission set out and obtained pre-approval for all of the images.

The artists are willing to discuss adapting their images to address your concerns. We urge you to accept SPARC's offer of mediation and to engage in a dialogue with the artists that is as respectful of their rights to free expression as it is of your civic concerns. By doing so you will demonstrate to the young artists that the free speech principles so central to our democracy apply equally to them.

Press Release

FOR IMMEDIATE RELEASE: September 25, 1997
CONTACT: David Greene, NCFE 202-393-2787

National Organizations Oppose Censorship of Mural Art by Los Angeles Recreation and Parks Commission

On September 25, 1997, twelve national organizations dedicated to defending the right of freedom of expression registered their strong objection to the Los Angeles Recreation and Parks Commission's disregard of the First Amendment rights of the spray can artists who created, with the Commission's approval, the mural in the graffiti pit adjacent to the Venice Pavilion. The groups urged the Commission to engage in a dialogue with the artists as has been suggested by the Social Art and Public Art Resource Center (SPARC), the organization which coordinated the mural project.

In a letter to the Commission, the groups challenged the Commission's assertion that the artists had waived their rights to prevent the Commission's removal of the images. The groups stated that regardless of whether the Commission acted legally in this instance, the Commission's blatant viewpoint-based restrictions are contrary to the principles of freedom of artistic expression as embodied in the First Amendment. The First Amendment prohibits viewpoint-based restrictions on artistic expression.

The groups, noting that the artists are willing to modify their images, urged the Commission to discuss the issue with the artists and SPARC: "We urge you to accept SPARC's offer of mediation and to engage in a dialogue with the artists that is as respectful of their rights to free expression as it is of your civic concerns. By doing so you will demonstrate to the young artists that the free speech principles so central to our democracy apply equally to them."

PART IV
Press Release Stating Position on Issue

For Immediate Release: February 9, 1998
Contact: David Greene, NCFE 202-393-2787

National Campaign for Freedom of Expression Says Funding Stipulations Would Unfairly Hinder Schools' Access to Arts, Other Materials

The National Campaign for Freedom of Expression objects to Senator John McCain's proposed legislation that would require schools that receive federal Internet subsidies to adopt policies restricting access to materials otherwise available on the Internet. Such legislation directly opposes the spirit of open and universal access that underlies the subsidy program.

"It is easy for Senator McCain to decry access to 'indecency' and 'porn' on the Internet. But what we have seen without exception is that the quest to block out 'porn' overreaches into materials that have significant educational and artistic value," said NCFE program director David Greene. "The arts has been hit especially hard in this area. Access to works by Picasso, Shakespeare, Mozart, Henry James, and other artists is commonly blocked by restrictive policies and filtering software." In its December 1997 report, "Faulty Filters," the Electronic Privacy Information Center, indicated that a filtered search for "Museum of Modern Art" retrieved only 0.2 % of the hits obtained by a non-filtered search. Numbers for searches of other museums and artists yielded similar results. Rather than "protecting" youth from "porn," McCain's proposal, if instituted by school boards, will deny our nation's youth the freedom to explore various diverse educational opportunities, and deny teachers the opportunity to assign research in a number of traditional areas.

Perhaps the most disturbing result of Sen. McCain's legislation is that schools receiving the Internet subsidy will be at a disadvantage to wealthier schools that are not required to adopt restriction policies. "Other school systems are permitted, within the bounds of the First Amendment, to decide individually whether or not to place limits on Internet use," said Greene. "But apparently the subsidized schools are not trusted to make these decisions for themselves. This is precisely the type of access inequality that the federal subsidy was designed to cure, not foster."

NCFE continues to suggest that policies restricting Internet access in schools be made by school administrators, teachers, parents and students based on academic criteria, rather than on the moralistic policing of local schools by Washington.

PART V
Protest Letters from Advocacy Organization

Sacred Naked Nature Girls

April 3, 1994

To: The President's Council of the Naropa Institute
From: Students Against Censorship

RE: Sacred Naked Nature Girls

As students and artists of the Naropa community we are insulted by the cancellation of the performance of April 17 of the Sacred Naked Nature Girls. The actions of the President's Council represent a significant precedent for our small and growing community. In a nation where political attacks on the arts are routine, the President's Council decision aligns our institution with the conservative agenda to keep art from being political. We as an alternative institution have a duty to provide a forum for alternative viewpoints, and not be limited by latent forms of harassment and discrimination. (See Student Handbook, p. 9.) To talk about experimental performance behind closed doors and then censor it with no option for appeal represents a breach of trust between those who manage Naropa and those who support it (both artistically and economically).

We do not consider the reasons given for the decision as substantial enough to allow for such an immediate action. If the credentials of the performers were in question, why wasn't a request made to the Writing & Poetics department for more information, or for justification of their sponsorship? If the politics of nudity is in question, we must ask why we support and advertise Allen Ginsberg, a true icon for freedom of body, mind, and soul. If nudity is not an issue then why was the potential trauma of rape and abuse survivors brought in as justification? If the use of the term "Girls" in the group's name is not considered appropriate nor feminist then we must question anyone who chooses to turn a derogatory term into one of empowerment, from gay's & lesbians, to people of color, to women.

The crucial point here is choice. They choose to express themselves the way they do, and we choose to support them. Anyone who doesn't want to see the performance for whatever reason is free not to attend. Each choice is equally valid. Additionally, the President's Council has now chosen to act as review committee for any performance at Naropa. This precedence has important consequences if it is allowed to go unchecked.

We call on the President's Council to invite the Sacred Naked Nature Girls back for a fully-funded and well-advertised performance. More importantly, we invite the council to engage in an open dialogue with the student body and public about censorship and the arts. We urge the Council to not continue making uninformed and rash decisions without consulting the sponsors of the event or the artists themselves. It is our hope that future generations and classes will not risk their cultural, ethnic, sexual, and artistic identities to administrators who are ultimately accountable to students and members of our community, in Boulder and around the world.

Students Against Censorship

WERS - Rap Music Issue

20 November 1995

Re: WERS - Rap Music Issue

Dear President Liebergott,

The National Campaign for Freedom of Expression is an education and advocacy network of artists, arts organizations and members of the public, founded to fight censorship and to protect and extend the First Amendment right to freedom of artistic expression. On behalf of the thousands of members of NCFE in Massachusetts and across the country, I write to express my deep concern regarding the decision by radio station WERS-FM to censor some rap music.

Silencing the voices of rap artists by banning certain songs runs counter to America's valued democratic ideals. Ignoring or banning their broadcast on WERS-FM only serves to marginalize these voices and further divide our nation along racial lines. Rather, we must listen closely to these songs to increase our understanding and to move towards mutual understanding.

The arts contribute greatly to the free exchange of ideas which is at the core of a democratic society. Not unlike community newspapers, the arts encourage debate and provide a public forum offering questions and answers to the many difficult problems facing our country. It is vital that the arts—ranging from rap music to theater to dance—are granted the same freedoms that our universities and newspapers enjoy as they grapple with the ever-evolving cultural landscape of our great nation.

The arts also serve as a catalyst for change. In challenging us to move beyond our own experiences, artistic expression serves to teach us about our differences and to bring us together as a community. Rap music, like other forms of artistic expression, is a vehicle for artists, our diverse communities and our nation, to replace fear and ignorance with understanding and action.

I urge you, as President of Emerson College, to defend the First Amendment by removing any content restrictions on music at WERS-FM. If the freedom of expression is censored, particularly where critical thought and higher learning are most encouraged and cherished, our constitution and democracy are at great risk.

Thank you for your attention to this matter.

Sincerely,

David Mendoza
Executive Director

PART VI
Letter to the Editor

Annie Sprinkle

The Seattle Times, Tuesday, May 3, 1994

Story on funding for lecture left out important information

The April 16 Times article regarding the de-funding of Annie Sprinkle's lecture at the University of Washington was inaccurate, misleading and omitted several important facts. Many UW students and faculty are outraged that four members of the ASUW Board of Control conspired to draft a false complaint against funding Annie Sprinkle's lecture.

Both the UW Daily and Seattle Gay News found the actions by the four BOC members newsworthy enough to give them front-page coverage. However, the Times article never mentions the four people or the bogus complaint.

In their rush to defund Sprinkle's lecture, the BOC members failed to do their homework regarding state obscenity laws that expressly exempt work that has "serious literary, scientific, or artistic merit..." The National Campaign for Freedom of Expression and the ACLU are exploring the legality of the BOC action.

The fact that this attack on freedom of expression has taken place on the campus of an institution of higher education is all the more disturbing. If our universities can no longer tolerate controversy and diverse opinion in the pursuit of academic inquiry, they will fail to teach students the core principles central to our democracy's survival.

Finally, as someone who has seen Annie Sprinkle's work, I am disturbed that the Times used a 10-minute section of Annie Sprinkle's 2-hour performance to characterize her work. The radical right, led by Rep. Robert Dornan and his allies in Congress, continues to attack artistic expression they find offensive by taking it out of context in order to malign artists and their message.

The Times' characterization of Annie Sprinkle's work is an injustice to Annie Sprinkle, the arts community and your readers. It serves only to provide a headline that Rep. Dornan can use in his fund-raising letters to once again attack artists, arts organizations and freedom of expression in the country.

Steven B. Johnson
Seattle Office Director
NCFE, Seattle

PART VII
Protest Letter and Press Releases by Organization

Out North Contemporary Art House

December 9, 1997

Dear Chairman Begich and Members of the Assembly:

The Board of Trustees, Advisory Council, subscribers, members, students, parents, artists, and other Anchorage residents involved in the numerous activities of Out North Contemporary Art House are very troubled by the Assembly action of November 18 to defund Out North.

The negative action of six Assembly members has resulted in many calls and letters of support for our work. We ask you listen to those who attend and are enriched by Out North performances, workshops, and exhibitions. It is *their* grant that you seek to eliminate.

Many Anchorage residents are disturbed by the process used to cut this arts funding. As referenced in the attached letter from attorney Hugh Fleischer, the mandatory criteria for grant evaluation was not used in the action to defund Out North. Additionally, this action was taken at a time when the Chair of the Arts Commission and others had left the meeting, believing that action had been postponed until December 9. These citizens could have provided the Assembly with answers to your questions.

In response to this Assembly action, the Municipal Arts Commission, at their December 1 meeting, voted to support their original recommendation of $22,000 for Out North. A letter from Commission Chair John Brower to Mayor Rick Mystrom explaining the Commission's recommendation is attached.

We would like to bring your attention to the attached letter from the National Campaign for Freedom of Expression, which cautions that "to defund Out North because of objections to the content of its programming, and without regard to artistic merit, is in direct conflict with the free speech principles so central to our nation's democratic and cultural heritage and exposes the city to substantial liability."

Several Assembly members have made it clear that their action to defund Out North is based on topics or viewpoints that they oppose, specifically those works which deal with gay or lesbian issues. We ask you to reject such government sanction, referring to a federal district court decision supported by a Ninth Circuit ruling that states: "Even when government is funding speech, it may not distinguish between basis of the speaker's viewpoint or otherwise aim at the suppression of dangerous ideas....Government funding of the arts...must be viewpoint neutral."

At least one Assembly member opposed funding Out North because its work is not suitable for children. The United States Supreme Court has recently rejected this argument by stating, "The Government may not reduce the adult population...to...only what is fit for children."

An Assembly member surmised that the majority of taxpayers do not want their money used to fund Out North. If that is true, what about the taxes collected from the minority? Do they then go unserved? If you believe that the minority of taxpayers in this city should not receive equal treatment through this arts grant procedure, please state your position so that we all know where you stand.

Gene Dugan, Out North's founder and artistic director, in a recent issue of the national magazine, Stage Directions, said, "Any theater company has to respect the values in its community, but there are many values, many communities." Out North serves many values and many communities, and it values those people it serves. In addition to my duties as president of Out North, I am a school teacher. In my work with children and families of many colors, beliefs and configurations, I teach the value of honesty, fair play, respect for diversity and the importance of listening to different points of view. These are essential values for a healthy city. I expect no less from my Assembly than I do from the children in my classroom.

We want the Assembly to listen to the people whose lives have been enriched by Out North. We request that the Assembly support the Arts Commission process that recommends funding for quality arts programs. We ask this so that the Board of Trustees of Out North will not need to undertake litigation.

Out North's Board of Trustees respectfully demands that AM 965-97 for grants to nonprofit arts organizations, including a grant of $22,000 for Out North, be approved by Assembly action tonight.

Sincerely,

Carolynn Lancaster
President, Out North

Out North 2

NEWS RELEASE: December 18, 1997
CONTACT: Carolynn Lancaster, President

Out North Gets 2nd NEA Grant in a Week to Expand Youth Program, Loss of City Grant Places Federal Funds in Jeopardy

Anchorage's award-winning Out North Contemporary Art House was informed today by the National Endowment for the Arts that it has been selected to participate in a national youth initiative to help make the nation's schools free of drugs, firearms and violence by the year 2000. In a letter to Gene Dugan, Out North's Artistic Director for Programs, Out North was made aware of the importance of this honor. "We are looking forward to working with such a dedicated organization," wrote Scott Shanklin-Peterson, Senior Deputy Chairman of the National Endowment for the Arts. Out North is one of seven nonprofit agencies across the country recently chosen to be a Demonstration Site for *Creative Partnership for Prevention*, a project of the National Endowment for the Arts, the U.S. Department of Education's Safe and Drug-Free Schools Program, and Learning Systems Group. Out North was invited to participate because of the nationally-recognized success of ON STAGE (Out North Student Theater Artists Gaining Experience), their innovative creative writing and theater program with at-risk teenagers in East Anchorage. "We hope to enhance the good work you are already doing with youth in the arts by developing a better understanding of how this work contributes to resiliency and drug and violence prevention," remarked Shanklin-Peterson.

Out North is to receive $5,000 plus technical assistance and training. A day-long training session will be offered free of charge for Out North's artists and community partners, including teachers from Clark Middle School and Wendler Middle School involved in their schools' Caring About Drug-Free Youth program, staff from Alaska Native Health Board's Trampling Tobacco Project, and peer outreach workers from Alaska Youth and Parent Foundation. Training will be provided by Learning Systems Group of Washington, D.C. with the support of the U.S. Department of Education's Safe and Drug-Free Schools Program.

The grant will enable the ON STAGE program to develop a model arts project that addresses tobacco, alcohol and other drugs and violence in the lives of young people. Thirty East Anchorage middle school-aged youth will be selected to work together over a two-month period to create a performance and present it to their peers and the public in the spring of 1998.

This is the second grant to Out North Contemporary Art House from the National Endowment for the Arts to be made public this week. Yesterday the NEA announced the award of a $40,000 Education & Access grant to Out North for the continuation of their ON STAGE program in the 1998-99 school year.

Neither of these grants replace the $22,000 Municipal operating grant to Out North recently eliminated by the Anchorage Assembly. These NEA grants must be used for direct program costs (primarily program artists' salaries and production expenses) and must be matched by local funds. The loss of the Municipal grant puts in jeopardy the nationally-respected Out North's ability to accept federal funds and Outside foundation awards.

PART VIII
Action Alert

Federal Way School Board Bans The GAP Theatre After Play Dealing with Homosexuality is Presented to Students

LETTERS AND CALLS OF PROTEST NEEDED

The Federal Way School District banned the GAP Theatre group from its schools following a presentation of "The View from Here," written by Carrie Gibson and Rick Turner and directed by Susan Finque. Two school board members and some parents claimed its treatment of issues relating to homosexuality, gender equity, and sexual harassment was "degrading to families" (*The News Tribune*, June 11).

School Board member Joel Marks stated in the June 5 Seattle Times, "They [the GAP Theatre] were trying to foist the homosexual mind-set on young, impressionable minds by making it an acceptable lifestyle choice." He added that he left the performance feeling "disgusted" and "physically ill." In addition, Board member Ann Murphy remarked that the performance "shocked and repulsed" her, stating, "When I left that assembly...I felt those holding traditional family values were the ones that were being mocked." The Christian Coalition of Washington issued a press release criticizing "A View from Here" for questioning "normal roles of fathers, mothers, boys and girls." Thanks to pressure from radical right groups, the GAP Theatre has already been banned from the Renton school district and from one Oregon school district.

Instead of defending free speech and students' right to hear and discuss a variety of viewpoints and ideas, Federal Way Superintendent of Schools Tom Vander Ark wrote in the June 18 Federal Way News, "We do not promote lifestyles or use material that does. Many people felt that the GAP production crossed this line and for that I apologize. They will not be invited back to the district. Our health advisory process is also being reviewed to ensure that we avoid productions that offend so many people."

Please contact the Superintendent and tell him that the school district should stop imposing censorship and sanctioning homophobia:

Thomas Vander Ark, Superintendent
Federal Way School District #210
31405 - 18th Avenue S.
Federal Way, WA 98003
Tel. 941-0100; Fax 941-8505

The Federal Way School Board members may be contacted at the same coordinates:

Gail Pierson (President)
Holly Isman
Linda Hendrickson
Joel Marks
Ann Murphy

Letters to the editor may be sent to:

Editor, Federal Way News
1634 S. 312th
Federal Way, WA 98003
Fax: 529-2324, E-mail: FedWayNews@aol.com

Editor, The News Tribune
P.O. Box 11000
Tacoma, WA 98411
Fax: 529-2324, E-mail: leted@tribnet.com

Editor, Seattle Post-Intelligencer
P.O. Box 1909
Seattle, WA 98111-1909
Fax: 448-8184, E-mail: Editpage@seattle-pi.com

Editor, Seattle Thomas
P.O. Box 70
Seattle, WA 98111
Fax: 382-6760, E-mail: opinion@seatimes.com

Bibliography

Censorship in General

Don Adams and Arlene Goldbard, *Crossroad: Reflections on the Politics of Culture* (DNA Press 1990)

Stephanie Barron, ed., *"Degenerate Art": The Fate of the Avant-Garde in Nazi Germany* (Los Angeles County Museum of Art 1991)

Pierre Berton, *My Times: Living with History 1947 to 1995* (Doubleday 1995)

Richard Bolton, ed., *Culture Wars: Documents from the Recent Controversies in the Arts* (The New Press 1992)

Varda Burstyn, ed., *Women Against Censorship* (Douglas & McIntyre 1995)

Moshe Carmilly-Weinberger, *Fear of Art: Censorship and Freedom of Expression in Art* (Bowker 1986)

Jane Clapp, *Art Censorship: A Chronology of Proscribed and Prescribed Art* (Scarecrow Press 1972)

Richard Criley, *The FBI v. The First Amendment* (The First Amendment Foundation 1990)

Joan Delfattore, *What Johnny Shouldn't Read—Textbook Censorship in America* (Yale University Press 1992)

Donna Demac, *Liberty Denied: The Current Rise of Censorship in America* (Rutgers University Press 1990)

Rajeev Dhavan and Christie Davies, eds., *Censorship and Obscenity* (Rowman & Littlefield 1978)

Stephen Dubin, *Arresting Image: Impolitic Art and Uncivil Actions* (Routledge 1992)

Janine Fuller and Stuart Blackley, *Restricted Entry: Censorship on Trial* (Press Gand Publishers 1995)

Ira Glasser, *Vision of Liberty* (Arcade 1991)

Edward de Grazia, *Girls Lean Back Everywhere: The Law of Obscenity and the Assault on Genius* (Random House 1992)

Marjorie Heins, *Sex, Sin and Blasphemy: A Guide to America's Censorship Wars* (New Press 1993)

James D. Hunter, *Culture Wars: The Struggle to Define America* (Basic Books 1991)

W. McNeil Lowry, *The Arts & Public Policy in the United States* (The American Assembly 1984)

Dave Marsh, *50 Ways to Fight Censorship* (Thunder's Mouth Press 1991)

New York Public Library, *Censorship: 500 Years of Conflict* (New York Public Library 1984)

Kenneth Norwick and Jerry Chasen, *The Rights of Authors, Artists, and Other Creative People* (ACLU/Southern Illinois University Press 1992)

Marcia Pally, *Sense and Censorship: The Vanity of Bonfires* (Americans for Constitutional Freedom 1991)

Charles Rembar, *The End of Obscenity* (Simon & Schuster 1968)

Jane Rule, *A Hot-Eyed Moderate* (Lester & Orpen 1986)

Dawn B. Sova, Margaret Bald & Nicholas T. Karolides, *Banned Books* (four volume series) (Facts on File 1998)

Dorothy E. Smith, *The Everyday World as Problematic: A Feminist Sociology* (University of Toronto Press 1987)

Samuel Walker, *In Defense of American Liberties: A History of the ACLU* (Oxford University Press 1990)

Samuel Walker, *Hate Speech: The History of an American Controversy* (University of Nebraska Press 1994)

Art & Sexuality

Bad Object-Choices, ed., *How Do I Look? Queer Film and Video* (Bay Press 1991)

Michel Foucault, *The History of Sexuality* (Vintage 1990)

Melissa Harris, ed., *The Body in Question* (Aperture 1990)

Gary Kinsman, *The Regulation of Desire: Sexuality in Canada* (Black Rose Books 1987)

Peter Lehman, *Running Scared: Masculinity and the Representation of the Male Body* (Temple University Press 1993)

Edward Lucie-Smith, *Sexuality in Western Art* (Thames & Hudson 1991)

Theo Sandfort, Edward Brongersma and Alex van Naerssen, eds., *Male Intergenerational Intimacy: Historical, Socio-Psychological and Legal Perspectives* (Harrington Park Press 1991)

Sarah Schulman, *My American History: Lesbian and Gay Life During the Reagan/Bush Years* (Routledge 1994)

Ann Snitow, Christine Stansell, and Sharon Thompson, eds., *Powers of Desire: The Politics of Sexuality* (Monthly Review Press 1983)

Carole S. Vance, ed., *Pleasure and Danger* (Routledge & Keegan 1984)

Pornography

John Caughie and Annette Kuhn, *The Sexual Subject: A Screen Reader in Sexuality* (Routledge 1992)

Andrea Dworkin, *Pornography: Men Possessing Women* (Plume/Penguin 1981)

Gordon Hawkins and Franklin Zimring, *Pornography in a Free Society* (Cambridge University Press 1988)

Walter Kendrick, *The Secret Museum: Pornography in Modern Culture* (Viking 1987)

Michael Kimmel, ed., *Men Confront Pornography* (Meridian 1990)

William B. Lockhard, Chairman, *The Report of the Commission on Obscenity and Pornography* (Bantam 1970)

Catharine MacKinnon, *Feminism Unmodified* (Harvard University Press 1987)

Neil Malamuth and Edward Donnerstein, *Pornography and Sexual Aggression* (Academic Press 1984)

U.S. Department of Justice, *Final Report of the Attorney General's Commission on Pornography* (1986, 2 vols.)

Linda Williams, *Hard Core: Power, Pleasure, and the "Frenzy of the Visible"* (University of California Press 1989)

Movie Censorship & Blacklisting

David Caute, *The Great Fear* (Simon & Schuster 1978)

Larry Ceplar and Steven Englund, *The Inquisition in Hollywood* (Anchor 1980)

Lea Jacobs, *The Wages of Sin: Censorship and the Fallen Woman Film, 1928–1942* (University of Wisconsin Press 1991)

Annette Kuhn, *Cinema, Censorship and Sexuality, 1909–1925* (Routledge 1988)

Leonard Leff and Jerold Simmons, *The Dame in the Kimono: Hollywood, Censorship, and the Production Code from the 1920s to the 1960s* (Anchor 1990)

Richard Maltby, *Reforming the Movies: Hollywood, The Hays Office, and the Campaign for Film Censorship, 1908–1938* (Oxford University Press 1992)

Merle Miller, *The Judges and the Judged* (Doubleday 1952)

Victor Navasky, *Naming Names* (Penguin 1980)

Periodicals

Index on Censorship

Artistic Freedom Under Attack, vols. 1–4 (People for the American Way 1992, 1994, 1995, 1996)

List of Plates

COVER

Donald Lipski, *American Flag Ball #3* 1990, installation at C.W. Post Campus at Long Island University. Used by permission of the artist.

FIGURES

1. LeAnn Mitchell and Barbara Bullock, *The Dream Deferred* 1993. Used by permission of Mitchell.

2. Marilyn Zimmerman, detail of contact sheets 1994. Used by permission of the artist.

3. Candyce Garrett, *Rapture* 1995. Used by permission of the artist.

4. David Swim, *The Heart* 1992. Used by permission of the artist.

5. Paul Mircea Goreniuc, *Space Dance for Peace IV* 1983, installation at artist's residence. Used by permission of the artist.

6. Mike Alfano, *Stand Up and Speak Out* 1997, installation at Nassau County Courthouse, Mineola, NY, photograph by artist. Used by permission of the artist.

7. James Bostick, *The Reclining Bacchante* 1993. Used by permission of the artist.

8. Steve Johnson, *Joshua in Repose* 1993. Used by permission of the artist.

9. Sharon K. Sinerius Rupp, *To the Democrats, Republicans and Bipartisans* 1995, photograph by artist. Used by permission of the artist.

10. Janette Hopper, *In Awe* 1994, from *Adam and Eve Suite*. Used by permission of the artist.

11. Jim Folts, *Thomas Lauderdale* 1992, from *Family Friends, & Neighbors*. Used by permission of the artist.

12. Jim Folts, *Karuna Neustadt and Lois Van Leer* 1992, from *Family Friends, & Neighbors*. Used by permission of the artist.

13. Jim Folts, *Marty K* 1992, from *Family Friends, & Neighbors*. Used by permission of the artist.

14. Marian Azbill, *Graffiti on the building next to the Round Valley Inn* 1993, from The People's Portrait Project, Mendocino in Black and White Collection, Mendocino County Museum, Willits. CA, #96-20-250.

15. Scott Church, *Hidden Heart* 1997. Used by permission of the artist.

16. Jerry Hooten, *Wishbone* 1995. Used by permission of the artist.

17. Beth Wesson, untitled 1996. Used by permission of the artist.

COLOR PLATES

1. Dayton Claudio, *Sex, Laws and Coathangers* 1992. Used by permission of the artist.

2. Maxine Henderson, *Gwen* 1995. Used by permission of the artist.

3. Marc Simmons, *Girls on the Beach* 1989. Used by permission of the artist.

4. Cecilia Alvarez, *Modern Living Through Chemistry* 1991, detail from altar. Used by permission of the artist.

5. Emerson Zabower, *The Philly Flasher* 1993. Used by permission of the artist.

6. Andres Serrano, *Pieta II* 1990. Courtesy of Paula Cooper Gallery, New York, NY.

7. Donnell, *Initiation* 1994. Used by permission of the artist.

8. Mona Waterhouse, *Letters Home III* 1992. Used by permission of the artist.

9. Richard Taylor (XPRES), *Piggy Man*, detail of mural located in Venice Pavilion (a.k.a. The Graffiti Pit) 1997. Restoration Project Coordinated by SPARC (Social And Public Art Resource Center). Photograph courtesy of SPARC, Los Angeles, CA.

10. Richard Taylor (XPRES), sketches for proposed replacement mural for Venice Pavilion (a.k.a. The Graffiti Pit) 1997. Used by permission of the artist.

11. Dread Scott, *What is the Proper Way to Display the U.S. Flag?* 1988. Courtesy of Wessel, O'Connor Gallery, New York, NY.

12. Ellen Zahorec, *Our Lady of Pysanky* 1995-98. Used by permission of the artist.

BACK COVER

Donald Lipski, *American Flag Ball #3* 1990, installation at C.W. Post Campus at Long Island University, after vandalism. Used by permission of the artist.

Acknowledgements

This Handbook was produced with generous support from

Robert Sterling Clark Foundation, Nathan Cummings Foundation, HKH Foundation, Albert A. List Foundation, North Shore Universalist Veatch Program at Shelter Rock, The Andy Warhol Foundation for Visual Arts, Ms. Foundation for Women, Endowment Fund for the Jewish Community of Houston, Astrea National Lesbian Action Foundation, MC Wray Charitable Trust, Heathcote Art Foundation, Vandam Performance Group, Working Assets Fund of the Tides Foundation, Art Matters, Inc, Glen Eagles Foundation, Allies for Justice/Funding Exchange, Henry van Armigan Foundation, The Norton Family Foundation, LEF Foundation, Washington Education Association, Jerome Foundation, Playboy Foundation, A Territory Resource, Joyce Mertz-Gilmore Foundation, Western States Center, David Geffen Foundation, Phoebe V. Haas Charitable Trust, Paul Robeson Fund, William Penn Foundation, Flintridge Foundation, Pequod Trust of the Tides Foundation, Ruth Mott Fund, Gordon Matta Clark Foundation, Robert Mapplethorpe Foundation . . . and all of NCFE's organizational, business and individual donors.

NCFE thanks the following NCFE staff, interns, and volunteers who contributed to putting this handbook together: David Greene, David Mendoza, Jean Fallow, Steven Johnson, Jennifer Wood, Bill Updike, Sara Mayman, Lake Perriguey, Bernadette Rodriguez, Travis Skaggs, Suzanne Foley, Carly Van Orman, Jennifer Fleck, Marie Hirsch, Minou Nguyen, Elizabeth McDaniel, Rebecca Levison, and Molly Luna.

Very Special Thanks to: NCFE Executive Director Gary Schwartz and all current and past members of NCFE's Board of Directors.